I took out the garbage because

I Love You

REFLECTIONS FOR REAL-LIFE MARRIAGES

Eldon & Carolyn Weisheit

CONCORDIA

PUBLISHING HOUSE

Internal illustrations by Carolyn Weisheit.

The Bible text in this publication is from the Good News Bible, the Bible in TODAY'S ENGLISH VERSION. Copyright © American Bible Society 1966, 1971, 1976. Used by permission.

Copyright © 1993 Concordia Publishing House 3558 S. Jefferson Avenue, St. Louis, MO 63118-3968 Manufactured in the United States of America

Library of Congress Cataloging-in-Publication Data

Weisheit, Eldon.
     I take out the garbage because I love you : reflections for real-life marriages / Eldon and Carolyn Weisheit.
        p.   cm.
     ISBN 0-570-04605-X
     1. Married people—Prayer-books and devotions—English. 2. Marriage—Religious aspects—Christianity. I. Weisheit, Carolyn, 1931–   . II. Title.
BV4596. M3W45   1993
242' .644—dc20   93-6864

1 2 3 4 5 6 7 8 9 10   02 01 00 99 98 97 96 95 94 93

Contents

As You Begin

Shortly after we were married, our church showed a movie about family devotions. It encouraged husbands and wives to read the Bible together and to pray together.

We tried it.

Over the years our family devotions have helped us understand something special about our communication—not only with God but also with each other.

At first our talking with each other and with God needed structure. We needed a time and a place—and a book. By following the books we learned the ways of communication. Now we don't need as much organization. We don't need to wait until the right time to talk with each other or with God. We see and feel the presence of God in daily events, and we recognize how much we influence each other's lives. We pray together at regular times, but also at times when God becomes a part of the conversation.

Please understand that these devotions do not all come from our own marriage—we're not that interesting. As a pastor Eldon says he sometimes feels that he spends half of his time getting people married and the other half trying to keep them married. Carolyn has provided the balance in his life that has made it possible for him to share in the struggles and joys of many other husbands and wives.

We offer these devotions as a way for you to have a three-way conversation—with each other and with God.

Carolyn Weisheit   Eldon Weisheit

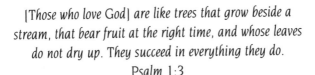

*[Those who love God] are like trees that grow beside a
stream, that bear fruit at the right time, and whose leaves
do not dry up. They succeed in everything they do.*
Psalm 1:3

● ●

A Plant Named Laurajohn

"John, look at what my Aunt Gladys gave us for a wedding present," Laura called as she carried a large potted plant through the door.

"Great," John replied as he kissed his bride and took the plant. "It's an ivy, right?"

"Swedish ivy," Laura said, "but that's not all. See, here's a yellow card from the florist. It tells us how to take care of the plant. Then here is a second set of instructions from Aunt Gladys. You read it, 'cause I'll cry."

John opened the card and read:

"This is a special subspecies of the ivy family called Laurajohn. It is the only one of its kind, because it represents your marriage, Laura and John. Each of you will remain the person you have always been. But something has been added to who you are. You, John, are a husband. You, Laura, are a wife. Together you are Laurajohn.

"This Laurajohn needs special care—and the care must come from both of you. You may divide other chores in your home between you, but the care of Laurajohn must be done by both of you.

"It will need water and plant food—not from one of you but from both of you. It will need to be turned and moved regularly—not by one of you but by both of you. Sometimes it will need to be pruned—by both of you. Occasionally it will need to be repotted—again by both of you.

"Your marriage makes you Laurajohn. It does not belong to one of you, but both of you. You will need to make adjustments, make plans for the future, learn from the past—and all of this must be done by both of you. Like the plant, your marriage cannot be divided into Laura and John. The two of you have become one. Neither of you can make a decision about Laurajohn by yourself. You're in this together.

"There may be times when one of you may have to ask the other to take care of the plant alone for a day, a week, or a month. But do not abandon your job without asking the other to take over for you. You will have to explain to your spouse when you are so busy, so tired, or so worried that the other must take care of Laurajohn. And you must be eager to again pick up your part of caring for the marriage.

"Talk to Laurajohn. Give clippings from it to your friends. Remember, it is a living thing and needs your attention.

"May Jesus always be present in your marriage.

"Love,

"Aunt Gladys

"P.S. I don't think either of you is superstitious. But if the plant dies, it says nothing bad about your marriage. Get another start from someone who got a clipping from Laurajohn or buy another one. Swedish ivies are tough."

Prayer

Lord God, help us take care of
the gift You have given to us
in each other. Amen.

Homework

Name a houseplant after your marriage.

How hard it is to find a capable wife! She is worth far more than jewels! Proverbs 31:10

● ●

Do You Want Me to Be Like Sue?

Mark and Gloria were discussing plans for the weekend. These were the nominations: a picnic and a ball game with friends; a movie and shopping by themselves; or just staying home together.

"Honey, do you want me to be like Sue?" Gloria asked.

"Be like Sue?" Mark reacted. "I don't get it." Married for three months, Mark was having difficulty adjusting his thinking patterns to new situations. He had always thought in straight lines—or at least long, slow curves. Now he found that discussions that required decisions often seemed like handballs bouncing off four walls, a floor, and a ceiling, as well as a partner's mitt.

"I mean," his wife answered, "would you like for me to dress more like Sue? Or do my hair like she does? Do you want me to talk like her?"

"None of the above," answered Mark. "I especially do not want you to talk like her. Why do you even think that I want you to be like Sue?"

"On the way home from the party the other night you said, 'Isn't Sue fun?' I thought you meant that it was more fun to be with her than with me."

"I didn't say that," the husband protested.

"You didn't say it," answered Gloria. "But I wondered why you said she was fun. I thought maybe you were trying to tell me something in a nice way."

"All I said, and all I meant, was that Sue is fun at a

party," Mark said.

"Then you don't want me to be more like she is?"

"Of course not," Mark answered. "Notice that Sue's husband has a job that puts him on the road half of the time. If you were like Sue, I would try to get his job."

"You're sure?"

"Look, I didn't marry you because you would be the life of a party. I love you as you are."

"I need to know that all the time," his wife answered.

"And I need the same thing," answered Mark. "It makes me feel good that you asked what I meant. If I ever say anything that doesn't seem right, ask me about it, please."

"Okay, and you do the same for me," said Gloria. "Now what will we do for the weekend?"

"Let's put two ideas together," suggested Mark. "We'll go on the picnic with our friends but skip the ball game."

"And spend that time at home," Gloria added.

Prayer

Lord,
You've given me a spouse—
With no instruction manual.
Will You please help me
Understand what's going on?
In Jesus' name. Amen.

Homework

Can you think of times when your spouse has totally misunderstood what you said? Did you tell him/her? Could it be that you have totally misunderstood something your spouse has said? How will you find out?

First Wedding Anniversary

Del was surprised. He had walked into his house after work to see his wife giving him the "sssh" sign and motioning him to follow her to the kitchen.

"What's wrong?" he asked.

"Nicole is upstairs," his wife said.

"Upstairs! What is she doing upstairs?"

"I don't know," his wife answered. "And she has a large suitcase with her—though she thinks I didn't see it."

"What is going on?" Del asked. "Today is their first wedding anniversary."

"I know that, but I didn't mention it," his wife said. "She just showed up. I asked her where Jack was, and she said she *thought* that he was at work. She said she'd like to spend some time in her old room. Then when she thought I wasn't looking, she slipped out to the front porch and took the suitcase upstairs."

"Was she crying?" Del asked.

"No, and she insisted that everything is okay. I told her I had plenty for her to have dinner with us, but she said she wouldn't be hungry."

"Do you think they've had a fight?" Del asked. "After all, this is their first wedding anniversary, and she shouldn't be coming home to her parents."

"I tried to ask questions but got nowhere."

Just then the doorbell rang. With a heavy lump in the pit of his stomach, Del opened the door. There stood his son-in-law Jack wearing a black tux and a sheepish grin—and carrying a corsage.

"Hello, Mr. Bronnell," he said with a wink. "I am Jack Evans. I'm here to pick up Nicole."

Del suddenly realized that he was part of an old re-run. This had happened before. Then he remembered. Nicole and Jack had picked their wedding date because it was the same day as their first date—her senior prom, the night they first met Jack. He remembered his lines.

"Come right on in, young man," he said. "I'll see if she is ready."

He turned around to see an amazed look on his wife's face and his daughter as she came down the stairs dressed in a full-length formal dress.

"There's a young man here to see you, Nicole," Del said. "But you're not leaving this house until I know what time you will be home. I've heard too many stories about your generation's ideas regarding prom nights."

Prayer

Lord God,
Bless the memories of our past
By making them a part of our present
And our future. In Jesus' name. Amen.

Homework

Talk about the events of your courtship, engagement, and wedding. What experiences should be kept as a part of your marriage? What rituals could you develop to keep the traditions alive?

*[Jesus said,] "If anyone declares publicly that he belongs
to Me, I will do the same for him before My Father
in heaven." Matthew 10:32*

● ●

They Won't Know How to Behave

"Before we go any further on these wedding plans,
there's something I had better explain to you," Becky said
to Don as she put aside the guest list.

"Have you found something in the small print of the
vows that scares you?" Don asked.

"No problem with the vows," she answered. "But
you are going to have to understand something—and I
want you to explain it to your family. All of you have gone
to church all of your life. You think of it as a part of your
home. Some of my family, and some friends too, have
never been inside a church building. They won't know
how to behave."

"Don't worry about your family," Don said. "My parents love them. And I do too."

"That's fine," she said. "But you all think of this
church stuff as normal. It's very special to me. My brothers think that I'm strange because I go to church with
you. One of my friends actually said that I am going only
to keep you on the hook—and that once we're married,
I'll quit."

"What did you say?" Don asked.

"I managed to say something about being glad that
both you and Jesus love me," she answered.

"That's pretty good," he laughed. "For a beginner in
this Christian stuff, you're doing great."

"But that's not enough," Becky said. "I'm excited

about my family and friends coming to our wedding, because they will have a chance to see what a Christian community is like. They think churches are like the television programs they've seen—and to them that's not good."

"So what's your worry?"

"I'm afraid they won't get it," she said. "I took my parents by to see the church yesterday. Mom wanted to check out the place for flowers. Dad saw the room in the back for parents with small children and asked me what it was. I told him it was the Cry Room. He said to Mom, 'Honey, they've got a special room for the father of the bride.' "

"That's funny!" Don said.

"And also dumb," Becky answered. "I don't want to have to tell my brothers to take off their baseball caps when they come to rehearsal. I don't want to have to teach them the Lord's Prayer before the service. Uncle Sid will probably light up a cigarette in the church and blow smoke in the organist's face."

"Don't worry about things like that, honey," Don said. "We aren't getting married in church to teach religious etiquette to your family and friends. We are asking both of our families and all of our friends to be happy with us. Jesus is one of those friends. I think He can put up with your Uncle Sid better than you do."

Prayer Suggestion

Pray for special needs as you plan your wedding or, if you are already married, thank God for the memories of that special day.

Homework

Talk about the attitudes regarding church that you learned from your childhood families.

As soon as [Adam and Eve] had eaten [the forbidden fruit], they were given understanding and realized that they were naked; and so they sewed fig leaves together and covered themselves. Genesis 3:7

A Honeymoon Story

The newlyweds met in the cafeteria after each had visited different sections of a museum.

"I want to tell you what I saw, honey," the man said, "because I think I saw us about 12 years ago. I was in the Greek sculpture section. There was a boy and girl there together—I'd say they were about 13. I first noticed them when we were in a gallery that had statues of women with no clothes.

"When the boy and girl walked in, the girl became very embarrassed about all the naked women. She was just slightly pudgy. As she looked at those beautiful statues I'm sure she thought she'd never look like them. But the boy was enjoying the scene. After all, it was art and he was there to learn.

"Then I followed the young couple into the next gallery, which had statues of nude men. The boy became very embarrassed. His voice was still squeaky, and he thought he'd never be built like those guys. Then it was the girl's chance to be the student of art.

"I enjoyed the shyness of that young couple, and I hope they keep it; because I think we have a little shyness together, and I think it makes us special."

"I'm glad you think that way," she said. "I was afraid that I would have to pretend that being naked together was no big deal."

"But it is a big deal," he said. "I know a couple who went to a workshop on sexuality. He said the goal was to become desensitized to the subject so they could get rid of their inhibitions. I don't want to be desensitized about sex. I think it is a sensitive subject."

"I'm glad we don't hide in the closet from each other," she said. "But I want your body to always be very special to me, and mine to you."

"You've met my friend Jerry," he said. "I think he could be a little more inhibited about sex."

"He might be more shy than you think," she said.

"Jerry?" he answered. "He wears shirts that open down to his naval and pants so tight that you can tell what kind of underwear he has on."

"But his wife told me that they were in a hurry to go out one evening; so she asked him to take the baby in the bathtub with him. When she brought the baby in she noticed he had put his swim suit on."

"Hey, Jerry may not be as bad as I thought," he said. "But I'm glad that you dress the way you do. You're beautiful and I don't want you to hide it. But I also am glad that I see a special beauty in you that is only for me."

Prayer

Thank You, God, for creating male and female. It was one of Your best ideas. In Jesus' name. Amen.

Homework

Are you comfortable with the way your spouse dresses?

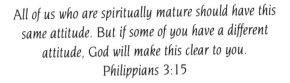

*All of us who are spiritually mature should have this
same attitude. But if some of you have a different
attitude, God will make this clear to you.*
Philippians 3:15

. . . .

I'm Not Your Mother

"Hey, honey," Frank called, "three stores at the mall are having sales on the kind of shirts I need for work. I sure could use some new ones."

"Fine," Maria answered. "The checkbook is in my purse. As long as you don't spend over 50 bucks we'll still eat on the last day of the month."

"I was hoping that you'd go shopping with me."

"I don't need anything," Maria answered. "I haven't worn one new outfit that I got at the last clearance sale. You're learning to be a good shopper by watching for the sales."

"But I wanted you to go along to help pick out my shirts."

"I'm not your mother."

"I know you're not my mother," Frank answered. "The last time I went shopping for clothes with my mother was when I was 14—and that was a disaster. I picked out red pants with a black and yellow shirt. She asked me where I planned to wear them. I told her church. She said, 'Then one of us must be changing churches, because I won't go to church with you dressed in that stuff.' "

"Then why do you want me to go shopping with you?"

"Because I bought that getup over my mother's objections," Frank said. "When I wore it I felt like a fireplug with a large canary on top."

"I remember the striped pants and flowered shirt you wore on our first date," Maria said. "You must have bought that by yourself too."

"Yeah."

"But I've never complained about how you dress," she said.

"And if you did I probably wouldn't ask you for help," he said, "because that would sound like my mother. But I'm the one who figured out that I might not have a good eye for color and that you do."

"Guess I had better go with you," she said. "But I don't like the idea that I have to tell you what kind of clothes you should wear."

"But remember that I asked you for help," Frank reminded his wife. "There are times when I need you—and I like that. By the way, there are times that you need me too. You would have fallen for the bait-and-switch deal on the microwave if I hadn't been with you."

"Okay," she said. "Remember that the clerk at the store will probably be a man."

"I know," said Frank. "And he'll be jealous because I have such a beautiful wife to help me and that she has such good taste in clothes."

Prayer

Holy Spirit,
Give us the same attitude
So we may recognize, use, and appreciate
Each other's abilities. In Jesus' name. Amen.

Homework

Tell your spouse what he/she can do to help you—and what you can do to help him/her.

You also must be patient. Keep your hopes high, for the day of the Lord's coming is near. James 5:8

. . . .

You Know Your Marriage Will Make It When . . .

1. You give each other storm windows for Christmas and think it was the best gift you got that year.

2. You both come home with the same flavor of ice cream that was on sale.

3. You agree that a Rottweiler is a beautiful dog and you would buy one if you could afford it.

4. You forget to watch the 10 p.m. news.

5. You pray aloud together and you discover that your spouse really does understand the things that are bugging you.

6. Your spouse gets a letter addressed only to him/her and you don't worry about what is in it.

7. You go on vacation and don't visit any relatives or friends.

8. Your spouse refers to the largest city in Florida as "Our-ami."

9. You spend Christmas in your own home rather than with either of your parents.

10. You and your spouse hold hands while shopping for a lawn mower.

11. You read the book that your spouse said was great. And it is.

12. You get a phone call from your mother-in-law, your spouse answers, but she wants to talk to you.

13. You start to ask a question and your spouse answers before you finish, and he/she was right about what you were going to say.

14. You have to take a trip by yourself and you find a love note from your spouse pinned to your underwear in your suitcase.

15. Your spouse buys you a new belt and it is two inches too short.

16. You find your first gray hair and your spouse tells you not to pull it out because it makes you look sexy.

17. You and your spouse invite a lot of people over for an evening and when they leave you both say, "That was a good party!"

18. You have family devotions together and realize that Jesus is at the table with you.

19. You look at a picture of your spouse taken 10 years ago and think, "He/she hasn't changed a bit."

20. You are happy as you drive to work and you are happy when you drive home.

21. You go out for dinner on a Tuesday night on a day that is of no special importance to either of you.

22. You and your spouse can both laugh at the way your families behaved at your wedding.

23. You have car trouble and neither of you thinks it is the other's fault.

24. You can read a book of devotions about marriage—and enjoy it.

Prayer

Thank You, God, for the many blessings that we have given to and received from each other. In Jesus' name.

Amen.

Homework

Add to the above list.

Be alert, be on watch! Your enemy, the Devil, roams
around like a roaring lion, looking for someone
to devour. 1 Peter 5:8

You Know Your Marriage Is in Trouble When . . .

1. Your spouse says, "Don't you remember what day today is?"

2. You invite six people from work over for dinner this Friday night and tell your spouse they are coming next Friday night.

3. You ask, "What's the matter, dear?" and your spouse says, "You ought to know."

4. You notice that your wedding pictures no longer hang on the living room wall.

5. You come home three hours late without phoning and your spouse does not ask, "Where were you?"

6. One of the kids asks, "Do we put a plate on the table for Daddy tonight?"

7. You walk through the bedroom nude and your spouse doesn't notice.

8. You come home and your key won't open the front door anymore.

9. There's a message for your spouse on your answering machine, and it's from a lawyer.

10. Your pastor phones and says he'd like for you and your spouse to drop by his office next week.

11. You have not said or heard the words "I love you" in your home for a week.

12. You go to the bank to add to your joint savings account and are told that your spouse closed it.

13. You don't laugh together any more.

14. You are afraid to talk about a problem because it might cause more problems.

15. You are at a party and are surprised that your spouse can take part in an intellectual discussion about the economic problems in Europe.

16. You compliment your spouse about a new sweater he/she is wearing and discover that it is old.

17. You can't remember the last time you had sex.

18. You find the dirty clothes you left in the bathroom in a box by the front door.

19. You find the "Dear Abby" column clipped out of the paper and pinned to your pillow.

20. You come home with a new hairstyle and your spouse doesn't notice.

21. Your spouse mentions an important discussion the two of you had last month—and you can't remember what it was about.

22. You come home from church and each of you thinks the sermon was exactly what the other one needed.

23. You notice all the good-looking people in scanty bathing suits at the beach and don't think about your spouse.

24. Your spouse wants to discuss an important subject and you say, "Later, dear"—but you never bring the topic up again.

Prayer

Lord God, help us see the little problems that happen every day. If we can't laugh about them, help us change them. In Jesus' name. Amen.

Homework

Add to the above list.

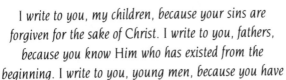

I write to you, my children, because your sins are forgiven for the sake of Christ. I write to you, fathers, because you know Him who has existed from the beginning. I write to you, young men, because you have defeated the Evil One. 1 John 2:12 –13

• •

I Know What They Will Say

"Your mother called today," Ann said. "They're having a dinner for Carla's birthday on Friday evening. We are invited."

"Do we have to go?" her husband answered.

"It's your family, and I love it when they all get together for a celebration," she said. "But it's up to you."

"Sure I want to be with Sis on her birthday and to be with the rest of the family," Larry said. "But you know what the dinner conversation will be about."

"Yes," Ann replied. "About the time they pass the green beans, your mother will say, 'Let's see, Larry, you and Ann have been married for two years and three months, and I'm still not a grandmother.' "

"Then Dad will say, 'That means that you won't have a child until after you're married three years—unless you have something special that you want to tell us now.' "

"I suppose we should just laugh about it, and stick to our own schedule," Ann said, "but frankly it's beginning to get on my nerves."

"I've tried to hint that it really isn't any of their business," Larry said. "But they both have the grandparent itch."

"My parents would probably be just as bad," his wife replied, "except they already have six grandchildren—

and two of them live next door. I think their supply has exceeded their demand."

"I tell you what we are going to do," said Larry. "We are going to celebrate with Carla. If Mom and Dad bring up THE subject, and we know they will, I'm going to look at you across the table and say, 'You know, darling, they are right. Let's go home right now.' Then I'm going to take your hand and we will leave."

"You wouldn't do it!"

"You want to bet?"

"No," Ann answered. "But it's going to be a fun family party. I'll call Jack and ask him to bring his camcorder. I think this party should be preserved as a part of your family history."

Prayer

> Holy Spirit, help us love our parents,
> Listen to their advice,
> And make our own decisions.
> In Jesus' name. Amen.

Homework

Do you think your parents (your in-laws) interfere in your marriage? Does it cause problems between you and your spouse?

*The message about Christ has become so firmly estab-
lished in you that you have not failed to receive a single
blessing, as you wait for our Lord Jesus Christ
to be revealed.* 1 Corinthians 1:6–7

• •

Communication Check 1
We Can Talk to Each Other

Ask a bride and groom, "What attracted you to each other. Of all the available males and females in the world, why are you going to meet this particular one at the altar?"

The most frequent answer given to explain spousal selection is this: We can talk to each other. And that's a good reason for marriage. The success or failure of a marriage can be explained by the communication between husband and wife.

Those who are planning a marriage, and the newly married, will tell how they spend hours talking to each other. They laugh (or is it bragging?) about their long-distance phone bills when they are away from one another. They tell about their first date when they started talking and hours went by like minutes. Then there was the time they talked all night—only to phone each other at work the next day.

Five years later the bride and groom are a husband and wife. They say they have a communication problem. They can't talk to each other!

Does it mean that they were wrong about the good communication before they were married? Had they fooled themselves into thinking they could hear and be heard?

Not necessarily.

In courtship the participants choose the subject of conversation. They can talk about the music they like, the food they eat, the places they want to visit. They can talk about comfortable things. Most of all, each can talk about self. Each is fascinated to hear about the other's childhood. Each feels honored that the other will share fears and personal pains. They can cry together.

Five years later they cannot talk about "I." The agenda now calls for "we." They no longer get to choose topics for easy, all-night conversations. They talk about necessities.

Some necessary topics are boring: Who will do the shopping? Have you paid the utility bill? Some are irritating: When will you do the dishes? Why can't you treat my family (friends) better? Some are embarrassing: What's happening to our sex life? Don't you care how you look anymore?

Communication starts at 101 level—and goes to graduate studies. Those who are beginners need to learn their lessons well and work hard—even when it seems simple. Those who think they are losing it need to back up and review previous communication successes—and try again on the more complicated subjects.

Prayer

> Holy Spirit, would You be my hearing aid?
> In Jesus' name. Amen.

Homework

On what subjects, and under what circumstances, do you communicate best with your spouse? What subjects and circumstances are the most difficult for good communication in your marriage?

For Christ's sake] I have thrown everything away; I consider it all as mere garbage, so that I may gain Christ and be completely united with Him.
Philippians 3:8–9

• •

I Take Out the Garbage Because I Love You

Sedona, Arizona—you've got to see it to believe it. South of the Grand Canyon and north of the Sonoran Desert, it is a small area tucked under the Mogollon Rim. Through it flows Oak Creek, in a rock-walled canyon of spectacular sights and echoes. The area is filled with natural sculptures that are measured in thousands of feet. In these wind-designed miracles of nature, people see the same ships and fortresses that they see in summer clouds. The soil has rusted and given the area the title Red Rock Country.

Arizona Highways said of this place, "If God hadn't made it, Eastman Kodak would have."

Sedona is our place of escape.

We go to be alone with each other, with our children, and with God.

Each morning I jog to find in the thin air a new scene of beauty, a new place of peace. And one morning I jogged to the city garbage dump.

A garbage dump in Sedona! A pile of trash in a place of beauty! Unphotographed, in the land of the camera, the garbage smelled and looked no different from that of Los Angeles or New York.

Why should I be surprised at the garbage? I had accepted the hotels, the shops, even the fast-food places. Garbage is the undigested leftovers of civilization. We study the history of early humans through their garbage.

As I look at myself, my spouse, our children, I can see the good. I can bask in the family vacation away from other responsibilities so we can devote ourselves only to each other. But I would be foolish to think that the luxury of our vacation did not create garbage for Sedona's dump. Even on vacation I take out the garbage because I love them.

But there is also garbage from our love, as husband and wife, parents and children. There are undigested leftovers of our feelings and our relationships. The comfort of our Christian faith says we do not have to hide the garbage. We neither photograph it nor deny it; we recognize it. I can't be a perfect spouse or parent. I cannot expect the others to be perfect either.

Paul gets to be called Saint Paul because he knew that his own garbage had been carried out by Jesus Christ. Jesus has offered me the same deal. He carries out my garbage because He loves me. And I can do the same for others.

Prayer

Show us Your love, Lord Jesus,
That we may become secure enough to love one another
In the same way that You love us. Amen.

Homework

Can one problem spoil all the good things that happen in a family event? In your family, who takes out the emotional garbage? Who removes the misunderstanding, disappointments, and anger from the family?

The peace that Christ gives is to guide you in the decisions you make; for it is to this peace that God has called you together in the one body. Colossians 3:15

* *

We Promised Each Other

As Rick rushed toward Gate 18 he heard the announcement: "Flight 463 to Dallas has been delayed. The new departure time is 5:45."

He looked at his watch. One hour to wait. He found a seat in a far corner of the lobby and was soon joined by another man who had been standing at the counter.

"Going home, or leaving?" the stranger asked.

"Going home," Rick replied. "The wife and kids were supposed to meet me. This will make it late for the kids. I hope she can get a baby-sitter."

"How many children do you have?" asked the other man as he sat down beside Rick.

"Three. You?"

"Zip. It must be nice to think about coming home to a full house."

"It has its moments," Rick answered. Then, looking at the other man's wedding ring, he asked, "Been married long?"

"Six years," the man answered. "My wife helped me get through school; now it's her turn."

"That explains the no kids."

"Yeah," the other man replied. "When we got married we promised each other we wouldn't have children. We're both career oriented."

"Was the promise for a while or forever?"

"For keeps," he said. "That's the problem. I've changed my mind. I really want children."

"What does your wife say about it?"

"I can't tell her how I feel."

"Why not?" Rick asked.

"Because we've got a good marriage," the man answered. "A lot of two-career couples that we know act like business partners. But we're lovers."

"Sounds great," Rick said. "Then you should be able to tell her that you want a baby."

"That's my worry," the other man said. "I know she would agree—for my sake. And that's not fair. We made the promise together. Her career would be affected more than mine. I can't ask her to have a baby just for me."

"But what if she has changed her mind and wants a baby but is afraid to tell you?" Rick asked.

There was a long silence. Two men, who didn't even know each other's names, shared the time as brothers bonded by a mutual understanding.

"I've got to talk to her, right?" the stranger asked.

"Sounds like a good idea to me," Rick answered.

Prayer

Lord,
Guide our decisions,
And our redecisions.
In Jesus' name. Amen.

Homework

Do you and your spouse need to rediscuss decisions already made?

*So then, confess your sins to one another and pray for
one another, so that you will be healed.* James 5:16

• •

Insured by Lloyd's of London

"We got another wedding gift today," Janice told her
husband as they prepared dinner. "It's from Ron."

"He's only three months late," Eric replied. "Maybe
his Christmas card will get here before Easter this year.
What is it?"

"There it is," Janice pointed. "He's your friend, so you
can open it."

Eric forgot about dinner and opened the package.
The gift was a salad bowl—plus a brown envelope with a
document inside.

"The nerve of this guy," Eric laughed. "Here is an application for insurance. No wonder he's always the top
salesman of the year."

"But look at it," Janice said. "It's for an insurance
policy on our marriage through Lloyd's of London. He
made this on his fancy computer."

"Trust Ron to be creative," Eric said. "After all the
identification stuff, he asks us to list qualities of our marriage that will make it last. Okay, me first. I think we can
talk to each other about anything. That should lower the
premium on our marriage insurance."

"And we practice our faith in Christ together," Janice
added. "We also have the same goals in life."

"Lloyd's of London should be glad to insure us," Eric
said. "But now the hard part: 'Please list those things
which are potential threats to your marriage. Remember

we investigate all policies for marriages that are insured for more than 10 years.' "

"Your friend is not very subtle," Janice said, "but he has a point. Let's start with the worst. The fact that I was sexually molested as a child will always be a problem for me. I was afraid I would lose you when I told you about it, and that fear will never go away totally. I hope you will always be as understanding about that as you have been so far."

"Ron probably meant this as a joke," said Eric. "But maybe we should write these things down. I have to list my alcoholism. You helped me through the treatment program and I honestly don't think I'll ever drink again. But there is addiction in my personality. We both will always have to recognize it."

"Ron knows about your drinking problem," Janice said. "Maybe he wanted to make sure you had told me."

"Could be," Eric answered. "But those things don't have to be threats to our marriage. The fact that we'd talked about them before we got his insurance application and before we were married tells us something. We can list our problems under ASSETS rather than LIABILITIES because we haven't hidden them. I need you. You need me. And Jesus will be at the center of our marriage. That's our best insurance."

Prayer

Lord Jesus,
Let guilt that has divided us
Bring us to the forgiveness
That unites us. Amen.

Homework

What should lower (or raise) the premiums on an insurance policy on your marriage?

Show a gentle attitude toward everyone. Philippians 4:5

Uncle Peanut

"It's fun to be back with the same old gang," Marti said as she and Phil shook the sand off their shoes and got into their car. The newlyweds had spent the day at the beach with old friends.

"Yeah," Phil answered. "We've known a lot of that crowd longer than we've known each other."

"But it is different to be with them now that we're married," Marti said.

"I suppose so," he said as they drove from the lot to the main highway. "What was different for you?"

"When we were a part of a group of singles we did a lot of teasing and used put-downs," she said.

"I never thought about it," he said, "but that's part of the fun of a group like that. We know each other so well that we can pick on each other without hurting anyone's feelings. In fact, I remember when Debbie brought you along for the first time. I liked the way you fit into the group and joined in the fun."

"And I liked the way you made me feel welcome by including me in the teasing," she said. "But it's different now that we are married."

"Did I say something to hurt you?" he asked.

"You got pretty rough on me when you told about the stupid way I pack a suitcase," she said.

"I'm sorry, honey," he said. "I didn't mean to put you down. That's the way everyone in that crowd teases each other."

"I know, and I tried to understand," she said. "But

the point is we know each other too well now. We're not just friends, we are . . . we are husband and wife."

"I guess it is different," he said. "I have to admit that I felt hurt when you talked about the way I eat soup."

"I'm sorry," Marti said. "I was upset at you and didn't realize that I was doing the same thing."

"But we have to be able to tease each other," Phil said. "We both have a good sense of humor. I don't want us to be serious with each other all the time."

"But I don't want to hurt you—or for you to hurt me," Marti said.

"I've got an idea," Phil answered. "My brothers and I—and Dad too—used to roughhouse a lot. We'd wrestle and tickle each other even though the others would scream and tell us to stop. That was part of the fun. But once in a while someone would overdo it, and there'd be a real fight. So we learned to say 'Uncle Peanut.' "

"Uncle Peanut?"

"Yeah," he said. "Uncle Peanut meant 'I'm not in the mood for this,' or 'You're overdoing it.' When anyone said 'Uncle Peanut' all roughhousing stopped."

"You mean that if we are with friends and our teasing gets too personal, we can say 'Uncle Peanut' and we stop?"

"Right," Phil said. "It kept us from hurting each other when we were kids, and we still had fun."

Prayer

Lord, help us be aware of each other's feelings.
In Jesus' name. Amen.

Homework

Do you sometimes hurt your spouse without knowing it? Find a way to tell each other about the hurts without adding to them.

Dear friends, let us love one another, because love comes from God. Whoever loves is a child of God and knows God. 1 John 4:7

- -

Children of Divorce

"Why are parents always such a problem?" Chuck asked.

"I think that when they get together, they say we are the pain," Lyn answered.

"But it's our wedding, and we have to go through all this discussion about which pew my father will sit in because we don't have a clue about who will be his date—and because, if she is under 35, my mother will be ticked."

"My parents are just as bad," said Lyn. "I've had to decide who will be the duty father to walk me down the aisle."

"But at least the step's and ex's get along in your family. I have a hard time keeping track of who is married and who was married, because they all seem to like each other. I still feel like I need to run my family through a body search before they are allowed in the same room."

"It's strange, isn't it?" Lyn said as she shoved aside the wedding plans. "We're both children of divorces, but we have such different experiences. I resent the fact that my parents were so casual about getting a divorce. They both went from one spouse to another like they were changing jobs. No big deal! At least your parents had the decency to hurt over their divorce."

"If you call fighting and yelling decency," Chuck answered. "I was glad when they got it over with because I didn't have to hear them battle it out all the time."

"Which is worse: To have a divorce because you fight all the time or because you ignored each other for so long that the marriage died and no one noticed?"

"Neither of the above," he answered. "And we're not going to let it happen to us. I'll be afraid if we argue, because it will make me think of my parents."

"And I'll be afraid," she answered, "if we get so busy that we write notes to each other and leave them on the pillow or communicate on the answering machine. I saw that kind of an attitude destroy my parents' marriage. They frankly didn't have time for each other—and didn't care."

"Let's compromise and learn something from our parents," he said. "To make you feel good, we'll argue one day a week—just so you know we're talking to each other."

"And to make you feel good," she said, "we'll have one day of silence each week. We won't even talk about the weather."

"And that leaves five days a week for wild, passionate love. We'll have a perfect marriage."

Prayer

> God, who has created
> The seen and the unseen in marriage,
> Keep us close enough to clutch,
> But not to clash.
> In Jesus' name. Amen.

Homework

With your spouse, identify two marriages that you both know as good examples for you. Then identify two that are bad examples.

So God created human beings, making them to be like Himself. He created them male and female. Genesis 1:27

She's a Woman

Howard watched his son and daughter-in-law get out of the car and come up the sidewalk. They were carrying Christmas gifts and food for the family dinner. The father could easily see that the young couple was having a disagreement.

"Hey, Rob," Howard said to his son as soon as all greetings had been exchanged, "I need some more tree lights. Come with me to the store?"

"As a veteran of 30 years of marriage, I think I recognize a husband-wife conflict," Howard said to his son after they were in the car. "Want to talk about it?"

"There's not much to talk about," Rob said. "She just lives a different way than I do—and it really shows up at Christmas."

"You two had some good counseling before you were married," Howard said. "You knew you came from very different ethnic backgrounds. And even though we may all be celebrating Jesus' birthday, we have a lot of different ways of doing it."

"Our different backgrounds, as you call it, has nothing to do with the problem, Dad," Rob said. "We are not having a heated discussion about national origins, racial backgrounds, or denominational differences."

"Okay. What's the problem?"

"She's a woman, Dad! That's the problem!"

"But you two have a great relationship," said the father. "I've seen your love for each other—and you are also best friends."

"All true, but the fact remains that she's a woman—and the difference between male and female is a lot bigger than that between races, nationalities, and religions. I knew women looked a lot better than we do, but I didn't know that their brains were different than ours."

"Sounds a little chauvinistic to me," Howard said.

"No, I didn't say we were better," Rob said. "I don't even think that I'm the one who is right and that she is wrong. It's just that we are different in how we see things, how we make decisions, and how we react to situations."

"You are 26 years old, and you are telling me that you have just now discovered that men and women are different?"

"Look, I figured out the birds-and-bees stuff before you tried to tell me," the son said. "But that's a minor detail in the differences between male and female."

"You're right, son," the father said. "You and your brother shared an apartment for over a year. You think about the differences—beyond the birds and bees—between a man and a woman as a companion for life. Then tell me how you feel about it."

The two rode in silence for a while. Howard parked the car at the shopping center and waited.

"Thank God for the difference," said his son.

Prayer

God, our Creator,
Thank You for making us male and female.
You know what each of us needs,
And what each has to give.
Help us share our differences
So we may be complete together.
In Jesus' name. Amen.

As for my family and me, we will serve the Lord.
Joshua 24:15

Bless This Family

This devotion is for your family when you move to a new home or once a year in the place where you live. It is not just a blessing of the building, but of the family that makes the house/apartment/mobile home/condo into a home. The readings may be assigned to members of the family. Everyone joins in the response.

Reader: Lord, we use this house as a gift from You. We ask You to live here with us. Protect our home from fire, burglary, and other dangers. Help us live together in love and peace.

Family: As for my family and me, we will serve the Lord.

Reader: Please be with us in the kitchen where we prepare our food and at the table where we eat. Make our meals a time for talking and listening. Give us food that is good for us, and help us use the food for our good health.

Family: As for my family and me, we will serve the Lord.

Reader: Be with us in the beds where we sleep. Give us good rest and pleasant dreams. Help us to go to bed each night with Your blessing and to get up each morning knowing that you are with us in the new day.

Family: As for my family and me, we will serve the Lord.

Reader: Lord, join us when we watch TV, play games, listen to music, and relax with one another. Guide our choices of TV programs, music, and books. Help us do things together that help us enjoy one another.

Family: As for my family and me, we will serve the Lord.

Reader: Make our home comfortable for guests. Help each of us be glad when others bring friends home. Help our relatives and friends enjoy our home.

Family: As for my family and me, we will serve the Lord.

Reader: Help us see how much You have blessed us as we look at all the places where we store Your gifts to us:

- The freezer and the shelves that hold food for us beyond today and tomorrow.
- The closets and drawers that store the clothing that we wear now and will wear next season.
- The boxes that hold memories in pictures, Christmas decorations, gifts, and letters from the past.

Family: As for my family and me, we will serve the Lord.

Reader: Remove from our memories all words of anger, unkind behavior, lies, selfishness, and other things that we have said or done to hurt each other. As You have forgiven us, Jesus, so help us to forgive one another.

Family: As for my family and me, we will serve the Lord.

Reader: Help each of us to grow in our faith in You, God, our Creator and Savior. Help us love each other at all times. Give each of us a good sense of humor, a purpose for living, and concern for each other.

Family: As for my family and me, we will serve the Lord.

Reader: Let all the blessings that we have asked for today continue to be on our hearts and minds as we receive them from You, our loving God.

Family: "May the Lord bless [us] and take care of [us];
May the Lord be kind and gracious to [us];
May the Lord look on [us] with favor and give [us] peace." (Numbers 6:24–26)

"Yes, I know," Elisha answered. "But let's not talk about it." 2 Kings 2:3

* *

He Won't Talk about It

Carla sat in her mother's kitchen—where she had spent hours with her childhood family. Now she was back, and only her mother lived there. She had another family miles away. That family thought she had made this trip to check on her mother. But she had come to check on herself.

"Mom," she said, "Walt is a wonderful man. He is a good provider. He loves me and the children. We go to church together. We have no financial problems."

"You came all the way back home to tell me what a good son-in-law I have?" her mother asked.

"No, I came to tell you that I'm thinking about leaving Walt," Carla answered.

"Does he know that?"

"No, he thinks we have a perfect marriage."

"Then why are you talking to me?" her mother asked. "You should be talking to him."

"That's the problem. He won't talk."

"I'm sure it would be hard for any man to talk about a possible separation," the mother said.

"I haven't even tried to talk to him about this," Carla explained. "I know he couldn't talk about a divorce. He can't even talk about plans for the kids' education."

"Do you talk to him about such things?"

"Sure I talk, and he says, 'Whatever you want, dear.' He agrees on everything to avoid talking about anything."

"Maybe he respects your opinion so much that he

thinks you are doing fine without him. Your sister would kill to get a husband like that after what she's been through."

"I know," said Carla. "Don't remind me of the ex-brother- in-law who knew everything."

"I can see how you are hurting, Carla. I don't know what to tell you, but I can tell you something about your father. For the first five years of our marriage we had an argument at least every two weeks, because he couldn't fix anything around the house. He tried to convince me that he thought a hammer was a nutcracker.

"I used to nag him about it all the time until I read something in a book by Peg Bracken. Isn't that strange that I remember her name? She may have saved our marriage. She said, 'There are two kinds of men: Those who fix things, and those who don't. If you married one who can't fix things, you can't change him, but you've got some choices. You do the repair work. Or borrow someone else's husband for the do-it-yourself jobs, or hire someone and send the bill to your husband. He'll be glad to pay it. Or you could divorce him and find a new one that could fix things—but heaven only knows what *his* fault might be."

"I'm glad you kept Dad," Carla answered. "But talking to your wife seems a lot more important than changing light bulbs. Walt won't talk to me."

"You have to decide whether he won't or he can't," replied her mother.

Prayer

Lord Jesus, help me hear the thoughts of my spouse
That are expressed not in words
But in silence, in actions, in feelings.
And help me talk about those things
That my spouse needs to hear. Amen.

Where, then, is the source of wisdom? Where can we learn to understand? . . . God said to men, "To be wise, you must have reverence for the Lord. To understand, you must turn from evil." Job 28:20, 28

* *

Help from the Past

"I was so eager to see you today, Doctor. Not anxious, but eager. See, I am learning. The last time we were together you told me that we had been spending too much of our time talking about the last few years of my life—since I've been married. You said my depression came from the past and that I'd have to look to the past to find help.

"You made me remember Collette. It seems strange that I had not thought about her for a long time. Collette was a year ahead of me in school. She was pretty and popular—but not stuck-up about it. She always had a special smile for me.

"I felt good because she went to the same church that I did. I would sit in the choir loft so I could see her during church. Then one time she told me that she liked to sit in her pew so she could look up and see me. She wasn't my best friend. I never went to her house and she never came to mine. But I was glad I knew her.

"Then her car was hit by a drunk driver. Her head was smashed against the steering wheel. She was in a coma for days and someone said it would be better if she died because she might be a vegetable. I visited her in the hospital—and she looked awful, but I still liked her. That's why I thought of her yesterday. When my husband came by I realized that I looked awful, but he still loved me.

"Collette gradually got better. She said God was her roommate in the hospital. She was excited about learning to talk again—as though it were a big adventure. She would laugh at herself because she couldn't tie her own shoes. She seldom felt sorry for herself, and she didn't seem to be embarrassed about her handicaps.

"Doctor, you helped me when you told me to look to the past for help. I had depressions even back then, though I didn't know what to call them. Collette would cheer me up when I visited her in the hospital—and later when she came back to school.

"I admired her, but it never occurred to me that I could be like her. God can be my roommate in the hospital here. I don't have to be ashamed of my illness. I can be cured and be well again—not just because Collette got well, but because, with God's help, I can get well.

"One time she showed me a little notebook that she carried with her all the time. She said her brain still had a few soft spots, so she wrote down things that she needed to remember, such things as names of people and her own phone number. Oh yes, this is something she wrote for me. I asked my husband to dig it out of my old high school box:

We never walk alone,
What more can we ask of the Savior than
To know we are never alone;
That His mercy and love are unfailing and
He makes all our problems His own.

Prayer

Lord Jesus, help me know that for every problem I have,
You are part of the solution. Amen.

Goodness is the harvest that is produced from the seeds
the peacemakers plant in peace. James 3:18

* *

Communication Check 2
Statute of Limitations

As a bride and a groom grow to become a wife and a husband, they establish ways of talking—or not talking. Most often they do this without planning. They just take the good and the bad as it happens.

But some simple communication rules help. The best way to avoid bad communication habits is to plan good ones. For example: Establish a statute of limitations.

First the problem: Some husbands and wives get in the habit of bringing up events from the past. These things seem to be unimportant to the other spouse; he/she may even have forgotten them. But the one who remembers and reintroduces a subject from the past feels it is important. He/she has carried the hurt for weeks or months. When a similar experience happens, the old pain is remembered and included as a part of the new problem.

Counselors call this "gunnysacking." Picture each spouse with a large gunnysack. As they live through the routine events of marriage, little irritating things happen. One goofs up the checkbook. One criticizes the other in public. One fails to give the other a phone message. One forgets an important date. One says something unkind about the other's family. The list is infinite—and that's the problem.

By definition these little thorns on the rosebush of marriage happen when both partners are busy. They don't have time to talk about it at the moment. But they don't forget it either. The thorns go in the gunnysack.

The little problems that could have been handled easily had they been discussed one-by-one all collect together into one big problem. When the sack is dumped out—and it has to be—the marriage is in danger.

The solution: Establish a statute of limitations. Recognize that it is normal for husbands and wives to do little things that irritate each other. But instead of waiting for pressure to build up to the explosion point, schedule a weekly time to empty the sacks. Pick a time when you have time for each other. Each spouse can then tell the other about anything that has been a problem. The appointed time is a speak-now-or-forever-hold-your-peace situation. You need not solve every issue, but all must be mentioned because the sack is emptied. The statute of limitations has expired.

The advantages of a weekly (or monthly) time to empty the sack: The problems are dealt with one at a time, instead of as a whole sackful. Also, both husband and wife have the time set aside to pay attention to each other and remove the problems. The problems are discussed on their own basis rather than as a part of another difficulty. But most importantly, both husband and wife have the secure feeling that their partner is not carrying a hurt. Both have forgiven and both have been forgiven.

Prayer

Forgive my faults that are carried in my spouse's gunnysack, as I forgive his/her faults that are carried in mine. In Jesus' name. Amen.

Two are better off than one, because together they can work more effectively. If one of them falls down, the other can help him up. But if someone is alone and falls, it's just too bad, because there is no one to help him.
Ecclesiastes 4:9–10

● ●

It Must Be Something That I Married

"Hi, Joan," Lucille said when she recognized her daughter's voice on the phone. "Are you and Jerry okay?"

"I guess so," Joan answered. "I just called to chat."

"I'm glad you called and I'm sorry your father isn't here," Lucille said. "You don't sound well."

"I guess I am worn out."

"Are you getting enough sleep?"

"Yes, Mother."

"Are you eating properly?" Lucille felt herself slipping back into the mother role.

"Yes, I'm eating all the right foods," Joan answered. "It must be something that I married."

"Something?"

"I didn't mean for it to sound that bad," the daughter said. "But it seems like our marriage has gone stale already. It's not like it used to be."

"You've been married for almost 10 months," Lucille responded. "The honeymoon's not supposed to last forever."

"We don't do the fun things we used to do, going dancing until two in the morning, long walks in the moonlight, talking for hours about life itself. Now we talk about bills and who will do the shopping and the laundry. He snores. Mom, you ought to hear it. And he didn't shave on Saturday; then he wanted to get cuddly, and he scratched my face."

"Is Jerry the only one who has changed so much?"

"No, it's me too," Joan answered. "I looked at myself in the mirror last Saturday afternoon—after I had complained about his whiskers. Not good, Mom, not good."

"You don't expect me to solve this one, do you?" Lucille asked.

"No, well, I just wanted you to tell me how to make it be like it used to be."

"I can't do that," the mother answered. "But maybe you're looking in the wrong direction."

"What does that mean?"

"Instead of trying to turn back your marriage to how it used to be, maybe you should work on changing what it's going to be."

"How do we do that?"

"Your father and I worked to put each other through school. Those were hard years, but we learned to work together for the future. We still benefit from the things we learned to do together then."

"We still have college debts," Joan said. "That's another pain."

"Do something together to work on the debt. Wash the car. Cook a meal together instead of eating out. Use the money you save to pay extra on the debt. Are you going to church?"

"Yes, Mother."

"Teach Sunday school together. Do things that help you see how you need each other. Don't try to relive the past."

"You make sense, Mom. Now I'll see if Jerry gets it."

Prayer

Lord Jesus, make us need one another. Amen.

48

*Let us keep our eyes fixed on Jesus, on whom our faith
depends from beginning to end. Hebrews 12:2*

It's Grandma's Anniversary

"I almost forgot," Leah said to her husband as they walked to the car in the shopping center parking lot. "I've got to get a card for Grandma. I'll be back in a jiffy."

"At last I've learned how long a jiffy is," Jeff said when Leah returned. "It's 16 minutes and 32 seconds. Now I always thought that a jiffy was shorter—the time it takes for a lamb to shake its tail or something like that."

"Very funny, husband dear," Leah said. "But it's not easy to find the right card for Grandma."

"I'm having a hard time keeping up on all your family dates, but I thought your grandmother's birthday was last month."

"It was. This is for her wedding anniversary."

"But, honey, your grandfather has been dead for seven years."

"I know that."

"Isn't that a little weird, no, I mean odd, let's make that unusual, to send a wedding anniversary card to a widow?"

"I don't think so. It's an important day to her."

"But it's for a wedding. Remember the until-we-are-parted-by-death thing? They have been parted by death. A card will remind her of her loss."

"But you never saw my grandparents together," Leah said. "They were very much in love. And just because he died does not mean that she can't love him anymore. She still thinks of him as her husband."

49

"If I died," Jeff said, "I'd want you to feel free to get married again."

"At our age it's different," Leah said. "But Grandma was married to Grandpa for 55 years. She doesn't want to start a new life again. She wants to remember the years they had together. So that's why I make a big deal about their wedding anniversary."

"I wish I had known your grandfather," Jeff said. "We lived so far from my grandparents that I never really knew them."

"My grandparents helped me understand what marriage really is," Leah said. "I needed them, especially when my parents got a divorce."

"But maybe it was easier for your grandparents," Jeff said. "In their generation people didn't get divorces as easily."

"Right. And there was a reason. Grandma told me that she and Grandpa had lots of problems too. But instead of talking about divorce they talked about the problems. When my parents had a problem, divorce was the first word mentioned. Then they couldn't talk about the issues anymore."

"I think this whole thing was a setup to give me a lesson," Jeff said.

"Maybe it was," Leah said. "But the next time we visit Grandma, you bring up this subject and she'll give you a lesson you'll never forget—not in a billion jiffies."

Prayer

Lord Jesus, help us build a solid marriage now so it will last until we are parted by death. Amen.

Let your hope keep you joyful, be patient in your troubles, and pray at all times. Romans 12:12

Family Weddings

"Aunt Bonnie, it seems so strange for us to be shopping together like this," Diane said as they sat down at a lunch counter for a rest.

"Why?" asked her aunt. "We are two brides who are getting married next month. We have the same shopping lists."

"But you are my aunt and . . . "

" . . . much older," said Bonnie. "Don't be afraid to say it. I'm 36 and getting married for the first time. That's not so unusual in today's world. By the way, you just turned 20, and that's young for a bride these days."

"Maybe that's what is bothering me," said Diane. "You have had so much more experience than I. You can handle all these details that make me feel, like, totally out of it. And you can pay for things yourself without asking your parents."

"Those are some of the advantages of waiting until what we politely call maturity before getting married," Bonnie answered. "I never thought about it until now, but I can see why you might look at my wedding plans with a little envy."

"*Little* envy? You and Alex are going on a three-week honeymoon to Hawaii. Don and I will be lucky to have a weekend at the Motel 6."

"Did it ever occur to you that I might be envious of you and Don?"

"Which would you like to have—our semifurnished apartment or the six-year-old car with payments still due?"

"Neither, thank you. I'm glad that I waited until 36 to get married. But I have to be honest with myself; I gave up something too. Alex and I will probably not have a 50th wedding anniversary. You will have many more years with each other. If we have children we will miss a part of their lives—and maybe not have much time with grandchildren."

"I guess no one gets everything out of life," the niece said.

"That's right," answered Bonnie. "We each have to make choices. Alex and I have some advantages because we are getting married later in life. We have talked about what we have missed by not being together during the earlier years of our lives. We know that we have each lived alone, and we will have a more difficult time adjusting to marriage. But we have decided that we are not going to let what we missed keep us from enjoying what we have gained."

"Maybe Don and I should talk to the two of you together."

"I think that's a good idea. We will enjoy being with you and seeing that you have things we have missed. Then maybe you can also be glad for us."

Prayer

> Lord, help us see what we have
> And not worry about what we don't have.
> In Jesus' name. Amen.

Homework

What advantages do you have because of your age when you got married? Disadvantages?

Let me hear your voice from the garden, my love.
Song of Songs 8:13

That Tone of Voice

Rudy was excited as he drove home. After three years in an apartment, he and his wife had moved to a real house. He and Connie were surprised and delighted that they could afford a place with a fireplace. Now, in the trunk of his car, he had wood so they could use the fireplace for the first time.

"Surprise, honey!" he called as he struggled through the back door while carrying three pieces of firewood. "Look at what I've got!"

"Where did you get that?" Connie asked. Rudy noticed a look on her face, and a tone in her voice, that concerned him. Was he dropping sawdust on the floor?

"I had to drop a package off for Paul on my way home," Rudy said. "He asked about the new house and gave us a house-warming present—a real one, because it's firewood."

"How much of that did you get?" Connie asked, in the same tone of voice.

"There's some more in the trunk," he answered, "enough for two or three fires, I hope."

As he took the wood inside Rudy wondered what was wrong. In three years of marriage he had learned to watch for "that look" and to listen for "that voice." At first the look and the voice had embarrassed him because he thought everyone could see and hear his wife's criticism. Later he discovered that this was one of the secrets of married couples. Connie also noticed "that look" and heard "that voice" in him. But it was their secret. No one else caught their private communication.

She was upset about something; that he knew. But what? Did she think that using the fireplace would make a smell in the house? But she was the one who wanted it. Maybe she wants to look at the fireplace but not use it. Could it be something unrelated to the firewood? No, he had seen the look on her face when she glanced at the logs in his arms.

"I assume that you didn't put the car in the garage," Connie said.

"No, I left it outside. We've got choir practice tonight."

"Then you'd better come with me," she smiled.

They walked into the garage and found one wall stacked high with firewood.

"Where did that come from?" Rudy asked.

"Our parents decided to go together and get us a housewarming present," she answered. "There it is!"

"That's enough wood to last us five years," he said.

"Or longer," Connie responded. "When I saw you bringing in wood, I was afraid you had bought another five years' supply!"

Prayer

Holy Spirit,
Help us listen with our eyes,
And see with our ears.
In Jesus' name. Amen.

Homework

Do you and your spouse need to write your own dictionary to define your body language? Try it.

Let us be concerned for one another, to help one another to show love and to do good. Let us not give up the habit of meeting together, as some are doing.
Hebrews 10:24–25

. . . .

We Have a Religious Problem

"Honey, do you get a little scared when you think about three weeks from next Saturday?" Marsha asked.

"Of course," Stan answered. "Men admit that they get altar jitters. But don't worry, I won't run, and you had better not either. I can't get a refund on my tux.

"I want you to look nervous," she said. "You're cute that way, and it shows you know what you're getting into. I think we have a religious problem."

"That's one problem we don't have," Stan said. "We grew up in the same church. That's where we met. And we'll be married in that church."

"Maybe that's the problem," she said.

"I don't get it."

"We've never talked about our faith," she explained. "I've assumed that you believe like I do."

"And I do."

"But I want to go to church—and I want you to be with me. I want to share that part of my life with you."

"I go to church with you," Stan said.

"Be honest with yourself, Stan," she said. "You go on Christmas, Easter, and a few other times when your parents or I think of a reason to get you there."

"But I go when I feel like it," Stan said. "I think it's wrong to go to church when you don't feel like it."

"That's exactly what scares me," she said. "If you are

going only when you feel like it, I know you don't feel a need for worship like I do."

"I don't think you have to go to church every Sunday to be a Christian," he said.

"I'm not talking about sitting in a building," she answered. "I'm talking about hearing God's Word, about receiving the Lord's Supper, and about being a part of a bunch of people who serve God."

"I do those things when I feel I need them," he said.

"In three weeks you are going to make a commitment to be my husband," she said. "Are you going to keep that commitment the same way you keep your promise to God?"

"What do you mean?" he asked.

"Are you going to be faithful to me only when you feel like it? Are you going to love me only when you need to love me, and not when I need your love? Are you going to take me for granted—that I'll be there when you need me, but you won't be there when I need you?"

"Of course not!"

"Then will you go with me to talk to Rex and Jane? I've talked to Jane about this. They grew up in different churches. Before they got married they had a difficult time, and they had to talk about it. Now they share their faith—not just on Sunday but all the time."

"When have you and Jane decided that we should have this talk?" Stan asked.

"We're having dinner at their place next Tuesday at 7:00."

"I thought so."

Prayer

Come, Lord Jesus, be our guest,
And let this home by You be blessed. Amen.

A fool doing some stupid thing a second time is like a dog going back to its vomit. Proverbs 26:11

• •

Don't Foul Your Own Nest

Some animals foul their own nests. Pigeons live in their own filth—and raise their young there. A mother hen, on the other hand, keeps her nest clean. Hogs are clean animals. It's the people who pen them up that give swine a reputation of being bad housekeepers.

Some people foul their own nests. The mess in their nests is not just dirty dishes and dirty clothes. The NEAT vs. MESSY contest must be worked out by each family. They should be concerned, not about winning the Good Housekeeping Seal of Approval, but the Good Heartkeeping Award.

People foul their own nests when they dump all their negative emotions on their housemates. Workers often bring home the frustrations of their jobs. Students bring home problems from school and friends. Instead of the home being an emotionally clean nest where family members can enjoy one another, they foul their nest by bringing the garbage home and giving it to one another.

Some adults still have leftover angers and fears from childhood. They bring the stuff that fouled their childhood nest along to their adult home.

Walk around your home and check it for emotional messes. Are the rooms filled with memories of anger, jealousy, selfishness, physical or emotional abuse, times of cold silence? Is your nest fouled? If so, clean the nest.

Good heartkeeping, like good housekeeping, requires hard work. You can't guarantee a clean house by promising never to make a mess. There's no point in having a home that you can't live in—and living makes a mess. Likewise, members of a family cannot promise they will never bring emotional problems home. We sometimes have to hold our anger and our tongues at work or school—then we turn them loose at home. Because we love the others at home, and because they love us, we can let it all hang out.

But whoever makes the mess must clean it up. If you said angry words, you apologize and ask for forgiveness. If you fouled the nest, you clean it. If another member of the family made the mess, you have to make it clear that you won't live in it. They may need your help to learn how to clean up emotional messes. But if you do it for them, they will never learn to clean their own nests.

Families need outside help to keep their nests clean. One of the best ways is to worship together. When family members join together in confessing their sins in public worship, they have taken their mess away from the home. When they are told they are forgiven because Jesus Christ died for them to pay for their guilt and rose from the dead to give them a new life, they receive love and happiness to take back to their home.

When one problem continues to foul a home, something must be done to remove the problem. Recognize the problem—as a problem, not a fault. We blame people for their faults. We help them with problems. Go to counselors, friends, those who have had the same problems. Deal with the problem outside the home.

Then come home to a clean nest.

Prayer

> Create a clean heart in me, O Lord, and
> Rebuild a clean nest for our family. Amen.

*One day Jesus was praying in a certain place. When He
had finished, one of His disciples said to Him, "Lord,
teach us to pray, just as John taught his disciples."*
Luke 11:1

The Lord's Prayer according to Us

Our Father who art in heaven,

We are lovers, a man and woman who have chosen
each other. In Your name we became one in marriage.
But we also have another unity. You are the Father of
each of us. In Christ we are also brother and sister. During those times when our love as husband and wife is
weak, use our love as brother and sister to pull us back
together.

Hallowed be Thy name,

May we use Your name as a reference? We want
Your name to be respected in our home, in the way we
speak about You and to You. We want our guests to know
that we are honored because You live in our home.

Thy kingdom come,

Please establish Your authority in our home. Be a
part of the way we use our time, our money, our lives with
each other, and the work that we do.

Thy will be done on earth as it is in heaven.

A big part of our struggle is to make "his will" and
"her will" become "our will." Help both of us to route our
wills via Your desk. Edit the wills of each of us so they fit
Your will; then they will also be our will.

Give us this day our daily bread;

Help us provide for our physical needs. Give us
those things that are necessary in our daily lives: food,

home, clothing, transportation, medical care. As we receive these necessities in luxurious abundance, help us see that they each have a special brand name because they come to us from You.

Forgive us our trespasses as we forgive those who trespass against us;

Each time I hear that my sins are forgiven because of the death and resurrection of Christ, help me hear also that my spouse's sins are forgiven by the same authority. Help us forgive one another not only as husband and wife, but also forgive one another in Your name.

Lead us not into temptation,

We recognize that our marriage is threatened by many outside forces, and even more so by struggles and weaknesses within each of us. Help us see temptation before it becomes sin. Help us protect one another from temptation, so we may avoid those forces that would divide us.

Deliver us from evil.

Protect us from car wrecks, fires, burglaries, layoffs at work, sicknesses, addictions, depressions, boredom, injustices, and all the other evils that would attack us.

For Thine is the kingdom and the power and the glory forever and ever.

Your power is our energy. Your glory is our vision. As we live now, help us remember the time we will live together with You in heaven. And as we think of eternity with You, help us see Your power and glory also with us now.

Amen.

It will be so. Not because we asked it, or because we want it, but because You have promised it. In the name of Christ we give You our praise and our petitions.

I may be able to speak the languages of men and even of angels, but if I have no love, my speech is no more than a noisy gong or a clanging bell. 1 Corinthians 13:1

Emotions: Utilities for the Home

The place where you live needs a roof, walls, floors, doors, and windows. But that's not enough. For your home to be livable, it also needs utilities; pipes bring in gas and water and more pipes carry away waste; wires bring electricity and receive and transmit phone calls.

But for a house to be a home it also needs other sources of energy. Emotions are the energy for a home, as utilities are for a house. Like utilities, emotions are not built into the house. They need to be brought in— and carried out. Emotions come in and leave, not through pipes and wires, but through people.

See your house as emotionally empty—not hooked up yet. It has furniture, food and clothing, and all necessities for physical life, but it has no feelings.

When people walk into the house they provide the emotional hookups. A person living alone has only his/her own emotions. The home may be a place of peace and joy, or a place of loneliness and fear. The lone resident lives with the feelings that he/she provides.

Those who are married have a duo hookup for emotions. One child makes it stereo. Each additional person in the house adds another source of emotional energy.

Check the emotional content of your home. First identify the emotions in your home without looking for their source. Do an inventory to list all emotions present in the home. Are there love, happiness, peace, joy, understanding, patience, and those feelings that make the home a comfortable place to live? Are there anger, depression, sorrow, bitterness, jealousy, and those feelings that make a home a miserable place?

Next, notice when the feelings are there: All the time? Some of the time? What events cause the emotions to become apparent? Are the emotions there only when a certain individual is present? Does the memory of that person activate the emotions even when he/she is not at home?

Recognize that each person living in the house brings emotions home. That is good. We cannot be human without emotions. We need to bring the good feelings of life home to share them with those we love. As good feelings are brought home they become a part of the furnishings of the house. Their memories continue to pay dividends to those who live in the home.

Your family might be tempted to tell each other not to bring negative feelings home. "Scrape off all emotional dirt before you come in and mess up the place!" Not a good idea. Home must also be a place where we can share our pains. We need to show our fear, anger, depression, and sorrow to those we love. But we can't keep those things in the home. Pipes bring clean water to the house, and pipes carry the waste away. So people must bring in emotions, and they must flush out the bad.

Jesus lives at your house. He is not an outsider. By His grace given to each of you, He supplies you with the good emotions and He carries away those that would hurt.

Prayer

Come, Lord Jesus, live with us.
Let Your love be our love too. Amen.

If you become angry, do not let your anger lead you into sin, and do not stay angry all day. Ephesians 4:26

Anger Is a Mind-Altering Drug

Ted parked the car in front of his home. He had been driving for over three hours. He couldn't remember where he had gone, but he was glad that he was back.

For three hours the same phrases had rushed through his mind, words that had come out of his mouth—words that he had said to his wife:

"I don't love you and I never have. I married you because I was sorry for you."

"I don't give a damn what you think, because it's not worth a damn."

"I'll call the lawyer in the morning and put an end to this crap."

He had called her names—names that he couldn't repeat even to himself. He remembered the anger on her face when at first she tried to fight back. Then he saw the fear, not just in her face but in her whole body, as she gave up defending herself and stared at his anger. He had left because he was afraid he would hit her.

Now he was back. The light was still on. He knew she could not sleep. She had no place to go. He had taken the keys to her car. He walked up the sidewalk, opened the door, and entered his home.

Crystal sat at the kitchen table. A crossword puzzle book and a pot of coffee were on the table.

"Are you okay?" he asked.

"I don't know. I can't feel anymore."

"I'm sorry," he said. "You have no idea how sorry I am. I can't believe that I said those things to you. I want to take back every one of them. I love you."

"Later, Ted," she said. "I've known you for six years and been married to you for almost two. I know you have a bad temper. I used to worry that you might be proud of your temper—some sign of your manhood. But it's worse than that. It's a sickness."

"I've been driving for three hours," he said. "I've repeated most of the words to myself. I tried to imagine what I must have looked like when I said those things. You've got to believe that I did not mean any of them."

"Then you have to accept the fact that anger is a mind-altering drug," she said.

"A what?"

"Anger alters your mind," Crystal answered. "I've seen it before, and I should have confronted you about it. I can accept the fact that you didn't mean those words. But you must also accept the fact that you need help."

"What kind of help?"

"You need to go to a counselor," she said. "And I'll go with you."

"I can stop it myself," he said, "if you will help me."

"No, I have let myself become a part of the problem. We will get help together. Tomorrow."

"I'll make the appointment," he said.

Prayer

Holy Spirit, Help us disagree without anger.
Help us to be angry without hurting one another.
Help us know when we need help from others.
In Jesus' name. Amen.

Children are a gift from the Lord; they are
a real blessing. Psalm 127:3

A Blessing Yet to Come

Dear Baby-To-Be,

You don't have a name yet, not even a projected birthday. But we think about you often—and find ourselves talking about you more and more every day.

You are especially on our minds today. We met for lunch, and at a bus stop we saw a young mother holding her baby. She appeared to be about 14, half our own age. We watched her as she held her newborn, no more than a week old. Her love for the baby was so obvious. She kissed the baby again and again. We could tell how pleased she was that others noticed her pretty little baby.

We know that young mother loves her child and will do everything she can for the baby. But we wondered how much she will be able to give. Will she give too much of what is not needed and not enough of what is needed?

We are eager to have you, our baby-to-be. But we want so much to give you what you need. We are not talking about the things that cost money. We are not waiting until we can afford you. You are far too precious to us to be delayed for financial reasons.

Our big need is to give you the love of both of us. We want to learn how to love each other so much that we know how to love you. We want our love for each other to produce you. We do not want you to hold our marriage together; but we want our love to add to who we are and what will become you.

We know it is easy to love a baby, one who belongs to his/her parents and is totally dependent on the adults who provide. But that kind of love can be shattered when the baby becomes a child, and the child becomes a teen-ager, and the teenager becomes an adult. Parents must love with a love that guides but does not control, that provides but does not own.

So we are learning to love one another without con-trolling or owning each other. Our ability to love one an-other will give us the kind of love that you will need. We are building a love between us that will allow us to love you with all of our hearts—and still give you the freedom to mature and be on your own because you will know that we have each other.

We like the system that God has given us. He gave each of us a need to love and be loved. We are growing in that love now. We do not make love to make you, but to make us become one. You will be the by-product of our love for one another. Neither of us could become a par-ent without you. You will need both of us, not only to produce you, but to be your parents all of your life. It is not just the love we will share when you are conceived that will help create you. The love we have for one an-other now will become a part of you. And the love that we will continue to have for each other as husband and wife will add to who you are, a very special person.

With all of our love,
Mommy- and Daddy-to-Be

Prayer Suggestion

Pray for couples that you know who want children and do not have any.

Homework

Write a letter to your unborn child or to one of your children.

66

Call to Me when trouble comes; I will save you, and you will praise Me. Psalm 50:15

We Have a Good Problem

"Don't you like my bouillabaisse?" Su Ling asked as she saw her husband pick at, but barely eat, his dinner.

"I'm sure it is delicious," Chee answered. "I know you went to extra work to cheer me up. But I'm worried. I usually can make up my mind and live with my decision, but this problem is beyond me."

The two sat in silence. Chee was working full time at a job he didn't like, but it paid the bills while he also went to school. In two more years he would have his engineering degree. Last week, to his surprise, he was offered a good-paying job in the field for which he was training. However, the new job would mean moving to another state, to a town where he could not continue working on his degree.

"I know I need that degree," Chee said, "but it seems silly to work at a lousy job while going to school, when I could be doing the kind of work I want next month."

"I made the special dinner because I think we should celebrate now," Su Ling said. "We need to be happy because we have a good problem."

"A good problem?" Chee answered. "Those two words don't work together. I'm going to tell your English teacher on you."

"But they do work together," she protested. "I learned that a long time ago when you first asked me for a date."

"My asking you for a date was a problem?"

"Yes, because I had another boyfriend—you didn't know about him. I told my mother about my problem, and she said I had a good problem. I didn't understand; so she explained. No boys asking for a date is a problem. One boy asking for a date is no problem. Two boys asking for a date is a good problem. It was much better to have a choice—and I chose you; so I don't have a problem."

"And my problem is a good problem because I have a choice?" Chee asked.

"Yes. If you want no problem, forget that you were offered the other job," Su Ling said. "Then we can be happy like we were last week and eat our bouillabaisse to celebrate. Or we can celebrate because we have a choice. It may be a problem to decide, but it is a good problem."

"But I can't just forget that I have the job offer," Chee said. "If I took it, we could have a baby next year and a better place to live."

"Then forget about school and take the job," she said. "Don't let what you have ruin what you could have if you want it. A problem is good when you have two good choices. You should have seen my other boyfriend. It was hard to choose because I liked him too. If I had made it a bad problem, I might have lost both of you."

"Su Ling, I need you so much," Chee said. "You make such good sense—and such good choices."

Prayer

God our Father, guide us as we make decisions, and help us see the blessings You offer. In Jesus' name. Amen.

Homework

Can you think of situations in the past that were good problems? Did you learn anything from those experiences that helps you make decisions now?

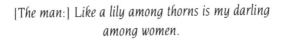

[The man:] Like a lily among thorns is my darling among women.

[The woman:] Like an apple tree among the trees of the forest, so is my dearest compared to other men.
Song of Songs 2:2–3

Reflections 1

I see me in him.
And him in me.
Are we a photograph of each other?
Or a mirror image?
Have we lived together so long that we look alike,
As often married couples do?
Or have we learned to balance each other
By being different in a similar way?
Do I scatter
Dishes, newspapers,
Tools, mail, clothing?
He does.
No!
I drape things—to hang them later;
I save steps by putting things here
So I can put them there when I walk that way.
I keep things visible
So I remember what must be done.
We each live by our own ideal of organization.
We have learned to lighten the sting of our
Nondiscipline by saying:
We deserve each other!

Reflections 2

I see myself
As a spouse.
I put myself on my own couch
For self-analysis.
Married only a short time,
I'm uncertain about who I am
As a marriage partner.
I am scared,
But amazed,
Unable to express my feelings,
But full of experimental trust.
My spouse is
(From my new point of view)
Exuberant,
Delicately in charge,
Eager for us to be a part of the same world,
Able to express love vocally, physically.
We both know gentle integration is necessary,
But our methods are full of errors.
Now we teeter-totter with our differences
And struggle to become one.

Prayer

Dear Lord Jesus,
Help us, so our temporary anger at each other
Will turn into a shower of love
Lavishly sprinkled on both of us. Amen.

Homework

Trade roles—that is, each spouse speaks for the other. Then discuss a subject that often causes difficulty between you.

*If your brother sins against you, go to him and show
him his fault. But do it privately, just between yourselves.*
Matthew 18:15

Dinner for Two at Home

When Dan came home he expected the noise of kids and the TV but heard silence. He could smell roast beef. On Tuesday night? He glanced into the dining room. The table was set—with company-best dishes.

"Hi, dear," his wife said. "You're right on time." She was dressed in the pants suit he had given her, with the earrings that drew attention to her beautiful neck.

"Did I forget something about tonight?" he asked.

"Don't tell me you've forgotten what day it is." She led him to the dinning room. The table was set for two.

"I should have brought flowers," he said. "But we just celebrated our anniversary last month, and your birthday is in March. Okay, what is it?"

"You'll remember," Katie said. Dan saw the wrapped gift at his place at the table.

"I knew I should have brought flowers." Then, aware of his wife's memory of dates, he said, "Let's see, it's the anniversary of the first time you drove a car. No, on this date your Aunt Thelma had her gallstones removed."

"Not even close," she said, "but the gift will help."

"It's a calendar—for last year," Dan said. "Good thing I didn't bring flowers. Last year's calendars are a bargain."

"Better check the date," Katie suggested.

Dan looked for this day and month in the year past. He read the notations for the week ending that day:

Wednesday: Argued with Dan about attitudes.

Thursday: Argument expanded to include the car we bought five years ago, his unfair treatment of my family, and my irrational behavior.

Friday: I told Dan that I don't like living in the same house. He offered to move out but slept on the sofa.

Saturday: I suggested a divorce. Dan agreed.

Sunday: Silence.

Monday: We talked about the kids in school and what we will do on vacation.

Tuesday: We made love.

Dan glanced up from the calendar. "Ouch!"

"We are celebrating that we made it another year. Look at the rest of the calendar. Our fights occur about every three months—always about the same things. That's the bad news. Now look at the good news. Nine months ago our argument lasted only three days. Six months ago only five days, but no one slept on the sofa. Three months ago we had four bad days, most in silence."

"You mean we're scheduled to have a fight tonight?"

"No, I mean it's time for us to change our pattern. Keeping this calendar has helped me. My goal has not been to stop the fights, but to make them happen less often and for a shorter time. And it's working."

"Yes," he answered. "We have done better this year."

"Let's keep a calendar together," she suggested. "That way we will both be responsible for having a good record."

"Does tonight count as a fight?" he asked.

"I guess it could," she answered, "as long as we get to day seven by the time we finish dinner."

Prayer

Jesus, do for us what we can't do for ourselves. Amen.

The truth is that Christ has been raised from death, as the guarantee that those who sleep in death will also be raised. 1 Corinthians 15:20

* *

Can We Talk about Funerals?

"Can we talk about funerals?" Andy asked as he eased the car on the interstate and into the center lane.

"We've got a three-hour drive," his wife answered. "If we start on funerals I hope the conversation goes uphill. What brought this subject up?"

"Remember I had to go to my boss' mother's funeral last week," he said. "I've wanted to talk about it ever since."

"I've never been to a funeral," LuAnn said. "What was it like?"

"Weird, at least as compared to my uncle's funeral at our church," Andy said. "It was at a funeral home, and the guy who did it obviously didn't know Mrs. Bernard or anyone in her family. Glen said he was a hired saint—he meant as in 'hired thug.' "

"Well, I guess that has to happen sometimes."

"People from the family—and others, I guess—got up and talked. The big deal seemed to be that she and her husband had been married for 55 years. We haven't even been married that many weeks. It made me feel like I was in the first grade again."

"What do we have to learn so we can last for 55 years?" LuAnn asked.

"I learned one thing that I don't want to do," Andy replied. "Someone read a letter that Mr. Bernard had written to his wife after she died. It was filled with a lot of nice flowery things. I guess you couldn't read anything else at a funeral. Then he said he was sorry he had been an inconsiderate husband and hoped she had forgiven him."

"I wouldn't want you to do that at my funeral."

"Nor you at mine," he said. "That's why I wanted to talk about funerals. I hope we live together for at least 55 years, but I'll tell you the good things and ask for the forgiveness as we go, rather than do it after you're gone."

"Okay, Andy. I like it better this way too."

"You know it's hard for me to talk this way, sweetheart, but while I'm on a roll I want to say one more thing."

"I'm glad that we can talk about such things."

"And I'm glad that we go to church and believe in Jesus and things like that," said Andy. "That funeral I attended didn't seem real. It makes me feel good to know that you could handle it if I died and I could do it if you died."

"I like that too," answered LuAnn. "But I'm still glad we have our seat belts on."

Prayer

Lord Jesus, help us live
As though death has already happened.
And help us die
Knowing we will live again. Amen.

Homework

Tell your spouse what you think about death, funerals, and burial. Then listen.

So [a man and a woman] are no longer two, but one.
Man must not separate, then, what God
has joined together. Matthew 19:6

● ●

Wedding-Ring Mobile 1

Make a mobile out of your two wedding rings—either in your imagination or in reality. Each of the rings can spin on its own as the mobile rotates. As the two of you watch the movement of the rings, you will see different views of your marriage.

First, see the rings as two separate circles, each hanging from the far end of their connecting rod. Sometimes marriages become that way. A man and a woman may be connected through convenience, habit, necessity. Their need for one another may be financial, social, or for appearance's sake. They are connected—but not directly to one another. What one does still affects the other one because each is connected to something that is connected to the other.

Often marriages start with a distance between the man and the woman. The distance is not seen by the wedding guests. It is not recorded in the pictures. But it is there. Some immediate need brought them together. Maybe one or both felt it was time to be married. They may have reacted to the pressure to marry from family or

friends, or they may have longed for stability. One or both may have felt a need for healing from a previous relationship.

There are many reasons why people marry that do not include the need for two to become one. This does not mean their marriage will fail. Their love and their needs must provide the energy to turn the mobile so the two rings overlap. Unless this happens the two remain two.

Other marriages start with, or develop, the unity of a man and woman as one. But forces other than their love for one another also spin the mobile, and the two who had been together move away from one another. The demands of their careers, their responsibilities to other people, and their own individual struggles move the man and the woman away from one another. The two who had been one become two again.

Sometimes the wedding mobile moves so slowly that partners do not notice that they have drifted apart. They may realize that cycles are normal in relationships. There are times when they feel so close that they are sure nothing could separate them. At other times they know their marriage can survive, even when they are distant from one another in mind and spirit, if not in body. They assume that the cycle will continue, but sometimes the mobile becomes a launching pad, and one spins into an orbit that does not include the other.

At other times a sudden event—a tragedy such as a death or a blessing such as an increase in income—can disturb the forces that held the two together as one.

Prayer

Lord Jesus, do not let anyone separate what You have joined together. Amen.

Then the man said, "At last, here is one of my own kind—bone taken from my bone, and flesh from my flesh. 'Woman' is her name because she was taken out of man." Genesis 2:23

Wedding-Ring Mobile 2

Husband and wife: Each of you lightly tap your wedding ring on the mobile. Even the slightest energy causes the mobile to move. Notice the motion: Each ring spins on its own axis, and each ring spins around the other. Because you are married, you are connected to another person. Anything that affects you will change not only your life, but also the life of your marriage partner.

Carefully move your mobile of wedding rings until the two line up exactly so they are seen only as one. When the sun and moon line up this way they create an eclipse. In a marriage, a man and a woman may also eclipse one another. The two become one—but they become one or the other.

In cliché views of marriage, a henpecked husband is controlled by his wife, or a wimpy wife is controlled by her chauvinistic husband. As in all clichés, there is a grain of possibility in these images. Some people look for a spouse who will dominate. Others look for someone *to* dominate. In all cases, both husband and wife are the losers. The one who is controlled loses self. The one

who controls loses the benefits that a partner can contribute to the relationship.

Sometimes marriages in which one partner dominates the other work—at least for the one who does the dominating. The two people may stay together, but it cannot be a healthy relationship. One is staying because he/she is afraid to leave or because his/her self-esteem is so low that leaving is impossible. The other stays in the marriage because he/she is in control. But the one who controls also loses, because the dominated spouse receives nothing from the relationship and, therefore, has nothing to give to the marriage.

At certain times one partner in a marriage must take control of the marriage. Sometimes one becomes incapacitated because of physical or emotional problems. The other must then make all decisions and provide for the helpless spouse. The one in need is fortunate to have someone to provide unconditional love and care.

Sometimes one partner in a marriage becomes temporarily entangled in work, in education, in a special responsibility. In such a case the busy one can hand over the job of caring for the marriage to the other spouse, but only for a while, and with the knowledge and approval of both spouses.

Marriage is a living relationship; therefore, it changes. Each partner must be aware of the changes in self and in the other.

Prayer

*Jesus our Savior, may both the giving and the taking
in our marriage be done in love. Amen.*

In our life in the Lord, however, woman is not indepen-
dent of man, nor is man independent of woman. For as
woman was made from man, in the same way man is
born of woman; and it is God who brings everything
into existence. 1 Corinthians 11:11–12

Wedding-Ring Mobile 3

Spin the wedding-ring mobile again. Catch the variety of views when the two rings overlap but do not cover each another. Notice that each view has three distinct parts.

First, there is the almond shape caused by the overlap of the two rings—this is the shared part of a marriage, where the two spouses have become one. Then there are the two crescents, one that exists only in his ring, and one only in hers. These crescents are the parts of their lives that remain a part of their individuality. The great mystery of marriage is that two become one, but they also remain individuals. They give themselves to

each other without giving up who they are. The almond part of their lives becomes greater because they are in union and benefit from what each brings to the marriage from the crescent part. The crescent part of each life benefits from the love and strength in the union of marriage.

Each husband and wife needs to know which parts of their lives remain under solo management. They may have their own friends, hobbies, relationships with extended family. Some have occupations that give little opportunity for the spouse to be involved. These areas remain a part of the individual. But the spouse is not blocked out of those parts of the other's life. Instead, from the individual parts of life, each spouse brings things of interest and value to the marriage.

Married people also need to define what parts of their lives are in the we-have-become-one category. Which friends, family members, hobbies, etc. become *ours* rather than *his* or *hers*? What can they share with each other about their work? Is their spiritual life a part of their marriage or their individuality?

For those who have children, parenthood becomes a big part of their unity. Most of their time, money, and energy are devoted to the family, all in the almond part of their lives. That's a good time of life, but the danger is that they become so involved in being Mom and Dad that they forget to be husband and wife. When children leave home, the center of their relationship is empty.

The mobile of wedding rings is always moving. The overlap of two lives that make one marriage sometimes becomes almost total, and other times becomes dangerously thin. The solution is not to find a balanced view of unity and individuality and lock the rings in place. Marriage is a living relationship. It must move as a mobile does. But watch the forces that make it move.

Prayer

Lord Jesus, You brought us together.
Please don't let anything or anyone divide us.
Amen.

When Jesus heard the news about John (that is, that he had been killed), He left there in a boat and went to a lonely place by Himself. Matthew 14:13

When I Need to Be Alone

There are times when I need to be alone.

This does not mean that I need or want to be away from you. It means I need to be alone with me. And I need to know that you understand the difference between the two. I cannot be alone with me if I feel guilt for being away from you.

I'm with other people all the time. I need to listen to them. I need to smile with them. I need to care for them. It bothers me at times that they get the best attention and energy from me, and you get the leftovers. I know that doesn't sound fair. That's why I want to explain it to you.

You are more important to me than anyone else. You are the one who makes it possible for me to listen to others, to care for others. You give me the security that allows me to take the risks of being involved in the lives of other people.

But I have to admit to myself that I have only so much to give. I run out of energy. My smile dies. That's why I need some time with me. I need a phone booth to change from being Superman and become Clark Kent again. I need a room, a chair, a corner, a place. I need that place to change gears. To become a spouse and parent again.

I don't want to come home and hide in the bathroom on the most uncomfortable seat in the house. I don't want to come home and continue to have the kind of relationships that I have with others in business and social encounters. I want to come home and start my evolution over again. I need to start again by being me. Then I can be a spouse; then I can be a parent again. I need to give something to me, so I have something to give to you.

I don't want to hide from you. And I don't want you to let me wallow in my loneliness. When I am empty I have no laughter and no tears to share. I cannot find a new supply in myself. I need you to lift me back up, to re-fuel my emotions again. Give me time to rest, but not too much time.

And I know that you also need a room, a chair, a cor-·ner place. Let me know when and where you need your time to be with you, so I will not think that you need to be away from me.

Prayer

Lord,
Help me know who I am;
So I can give me to my family.
In Jesus' name. Amen.

Homework

Find a place in your home for each of you to be alone. Respect each other's privacy when you are in that place.

Everything that happens in this world happens at the time God chooses. . . . [He sets] the time for making love and the time for not making love, the time for kissing and the time for not kissing. Ecclesiastes 3:1, 5

Wedding Anniversary Memories

The First Anniversary

I used to think
    That darkened streets
    Were lonely, lifeless, dull.
I used to think
    That all the fun
        Was in parties, laughter, lights.
But now I know.

The Third Anniversary

The roses would be dead
While the bill's still due;
So this year a poem
Must say, "I love you."

The Sixth Anniversary

A day unmolested by Hallmark,
Forgotten by all but closest family,
On a Tuesday, lost in a week of work,
No clue for a special gift.
But an important day in our history.
Mountains must be separated by valleys.

The Tenth Anniversary

Two weeks away from kids,
    Jobs, and household chores.
We talk—two hours at breakfast,

While riding buses on which
No one else understands English.
(We hope.)
We talk—and you say,
    "But that's what I used to say!"
And I say,
    "But that's what I used to say!"
In 10 years have we moved so close
        that we have passed one another?
In another 10 years
    Will we be exactly alike?
We hope not!

A Future Anniversary

(Planning for the traditional mid-life crisis.)
Secure in the love of wife,
        Children, and parents;
Secure in the love of Christ
        And a fellowship of Christian people;
I take the plunge!
I jump deep into all my fantasies—
        Wealth, power, sex, fame, and revenge.
They march through my mind
        In glorious array.
It was a fantastic trip to fantasy.
It was a real trip back to realities.
And I learned—
        That my realities
        Are better than my fantasies.

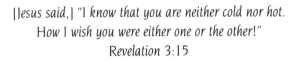

[Jesus said,] "I know that you are neither cold nor hot.
How I wish you were either one or the other!"
Revelation 3:15

The Fifth Wedding Anniversary

"What do you want to do for our anniversary?" Karla asked as she and John drove back from a weekend with her parents.

"We've done dinner and a movie for the last three years," John said. "Are we getting into a rut?"

"It's been fun," she said. "Maybe I'm getting old, but I enjoy just being together without lots of people."

"Me too," John said. "I was thinking about our anniversary on the way to work last week. We've had some great things happen in five years."

"The most important is sleeping in the back," Karla said, pointing to their daughter in the car seat. "And I like our home too."

"We've both finished school during those five years," he added. "But we've had some bad times too. I think we've solved the problem of our jealousy. We've got to admit that it has been a problem."

"Yes," she answered. "And the need each of us has to control the other. I hope we can do better."

"It's easy to talk about now," John said. "But I think we've got a way to go on that one. You want to drive?"

"No—only because I'm sure you can't get lost between here and home," she smiled.

"Back to my anniversary reveries," he said. "I realized that the problems we are talking about, and a few others, will never be a threat to our marriage for the simple reason that we are talking about them."

"Does that mean we are home free?"

"No," John said. "The biggest threat to our marriage could be the blahs."

"The blahs?"

"That's it. We know how to have fun together. I think we handle our conflicts better than most. It's the in-between times that could kill us. I mean the times when we are busy doing the routine things that don't involve each other—and the things that we don't have to talk about with each other."

"That's what happened to Bert and Janet," Karla answered, referring to her sister and brother-in-law. "They're so bored with life and with each other that they can't even find the energy to get a divorce."

"Yeah," he said, "and my parents are getting that way too."

"Are we doing it?" she asked.

"I hope not, but I think we should do something to keep life interesting."

"Does that mean we have to stay out late dancing on our anniversary?"

"No, we've got to go deeper than that," he answered. "We could take a course together at the community college as our present to each other."

"Or we could team-teach Sunday school," she suggested. "A bunch of third graders would help us realize that our baby will soon be a little girl."

"Let's talk about it over dinner on our anniversary."

"And be real radical by skipping the movie."

Prayer

Lord Jesus, don't let us lose the joy that we have found in each other. Amen.

There is no fear in love; perfect love drives out all fear. So then, love has not been made perfect in anyone who is afraid, because fear has to do with punishment.
1 John 4:18

Dinner for 12

Cindy was content. She sat as a guest at a dinner table with 11 other people, her husband, Chuck, seated across from her, and five other couples. Next Tuesday she and her husband would celebrate their third wedding anniversary. They had great plans for the evening.

She glanced around the table. The conversation was lively enough that she could drop out and just watch without being missed in the dialog. Three years ago she and Chuck did not know any of these people. Now they were "our" friends—not his, not hers, but ours. Two of the couples were from their church, one from the neighborhood, and they had met the other two through friends.

Cindy thought about how much easier it had been than she had expected. To get married, move to a new city, and start a new job all at the same time could have been a problem. But it wasn't—and she knew why. Chuck made it easy for her. She knew that she had helped him too. That made it even better.

Dinner was delicious, but now it was time for dessert. She wondered what she should do. The scales told her she had gained 13 pounds since getting married. And the way her clothes fit, she knew she could not argue with the evidence. But the dessert was homemade pecan pie, so once more she told herself she would start cutting back on calories tomorrow. But she declined the ice cream that was offered with the pie.

She listened to Chuck as he told a story about their courtship. It was a funny story and kind of romantic. She liked the way he told it. She wondered if he had noticed that she had gained weight. He never said anything. She had hinted by saying something about the way her pants and sweater fit as they got dressed that evening. He told her she looked great—and she wanted to believe it.

"Would anyone like another piece of pie?" the hostess asked. "I've got another pie in the kitchen, and it is already cut."

"Not for my wife," Chuck said. "She's gaining too much weight."

"Since it is already cut, I'd like another piece," said Cindy. "And this time I'll take just a small scoop of ice cream."

Prayer

Lord,
Teach me to give compliments publicly,
Criticism privately,
And to gripe not at all.
In Jesus' name. Amen.

Homework

Have you hurt your spouse by the way you have spoken publicly about him/her? Have you been hurt by your spouse's public criticism?

If we say that we have no sin, we deceive ourselves, and there is no truth in us. But if we confess our sins to God, He will keep His promise and do what is right: He will forgive us our sins and purify us from all our wrongdoing. 1 John 1:8–9

It Wasn't Real to Me

Sally and Jeff told their friends good-bye and walked across the parking lot to their car. At their friends' invitation they had just attended an evening seminar on family values.

"What did you think about it?" Sally asked.

"I guess it was okay," Jeff answered. "I can't disagree with anything that was said."

"It wasn't real to me," she said. "In the movie every family lived in a beautiful home with lovely furniture. They all had perfect children, and at least one boy and one girl. They all ate meals as though they expected the Queen of England to show up."

"See, I was feeling guilty because we don't measure up," Jeff said. "But maybe we're okay, because I had the same reaction. All those testimonies from perfect families gave me social diabetes."

"We sound as though we always want to live in a messy place and have a fight every week."

"No, I want our marriage to improve," he said. "That's why I went tonight. But I want it to be real. My parents always pretended everything was okay. My mother would yell at Dad, or us kids, with a tone of voice that sounded like she was a radio announcer for a boxing match; then she'd answer the phone with a sweet 'helllloo00,' and sound like Scarlett O'Hara eating honey. I didn't like it."

"You mean you don't want me to yell at you?"

"No, I can handle that. Dad deserved it once in a while, and I probably did then and do now. But I want to be real about it. I'm not a perfect husband, and you're not a perfect wife. I can live with that. But I don't want to pretend that we are like the people we heard tonight."

"But some of my friends think our marriage is a little unreal," Sally said.

"Why?"

"Because we go to church together and have devotions at home together every day. Glenda said she can't see how we can pray together at night and then have sex."

"Tell her that we are praying that everything works right and that our prayers have been answered."

"Oh, I know her elevator got stuck on the 'life-is-a-pain' floor," Sally said. "But I think we are special because we are honest with each other about both the good and bad things in our marriage. I hope we never lose it."

"Let's lead a seminar called 'Living Like It Really Is.'"

"Okay, but you go first," Sally said. "And I'll sit in the back row to hear what you say—and I just might walk out."

Prayer

Jesus our friend,
Help us love each other
The way You love each of us. Amen.

Homework

Name other couples who have the kind of marriage that is a good example for you.

Be faithful to your own wife and give your love
to her alone. Proverbs 5:15

* *

I Think He's Unfaithful

"Were you comfortable with my friends?" Mario asked his wife of three months after they had attended a company picnic.

"Sure," Dinah answered. "But remember, I didn't know anyone in this city when we got married, and you have lots of friends here."

"That's why I asked."

"I really enjoyed the Glassers," she said. "I think that Joan will become my friend, but to be honest I'm not comfortable around the Bronsons."

"Why not?" asked Mario.

"I think Larry is unfaithful to his wife," Dinah said.

"He may be a jerk—I'll admit that—but I don't think he messes around."

"I didn't mean that he was unfaithful to her with other women," she explained.

"There are other ways to be unfaithful?"

"Sure, lots of ways," she answered. "I think Larry is unfaithful to his wife intellectually. We were talking about the environmental problems in South America. Kathy told about an article she had read, and Larry ridiculed her opinion. I think she knows more about the subject than he does."

"That's unfaithful?"

"Yes, it is," Dinah answered. "He could have disagreed with her, if he knew something about the subject.

But he just put her down as though her opinion was worthless."

"I heard him do the same thing when she mentioned Senator Robert's speech," Mario said.

"He is also unfaithful to her regarding her work. Someone asked what she did, and as she was explaining Larry said, 'Anybody can do what she does.' "

"I have always known that Larry was kind of shallow, but he may be worse than I thought," Mario said. "Do you think I am faithful to you?"

"Yes," Dinah said. "In all ways."

"That's what I promised you."

"And that's what I promised you."

"But you're making it more complicated," he mentioned. "I know I won't be unfaithful to you sexually. I thought that was it."

"But isn't it fun to know that I'll be faithful to you in all the other ways too?" she asked.

"Yeah," he answered. "Does this mean that we have to go say our vows again, so I get it right?"

"No," Dinah answered. "I believed you the first time. But I think it's a good idea for us to check up on how we're doing with those vows every now and then."

"Okay, we've done it now," Mario said. "You let me know when it's then."

Prayer

Lord Jesus,
Help us be faithful to one another
In body, mind, and spirit. Amen.

Homework

Talk to each other about being faithful. What does it mean to be faithful to each other? to parents? to children? to God?

*A person's thoughts are like water in a deep well, but
someone with insight can draw them out.* Proverbs 20:5

* *

The Sky Is Falling

Marsha was an hour late coming home from work. When she walked into the kitchen, Ron had dinner on the table and a worried and/or angry look on his face.

"Don't even ask what kind of a day I had," she said.

"I've been married long enough to know that means I should ask," her husband responded. "So how was your day?"

"Since you really want to know—lousy," she said. "MISTER Rothwell spent all day practicing his new method of administration, which we call make-everyone-suspicious-of-everyone-else. The new guy Dale who works for me came in an hour late and told me that he was up all night with the baby, and since I am a woman he knew I would understand. The whole computer system applied for early retirement."

Ron listened. Earlier in their short marriage he had tried to solve each problem that his wife brought home from work. But he had discovered that his solutions caused bigger problems.

"When I was on the elevator going down after work," Marsha continued, "I said to myself, 'At least I made it through the day without snagging my pantyhose.' Then I got to the car and one tire was flat—I mean flat-out flat. That put me over the limit of my emotional credit. My first thought was about you, dear husband. I was angry because you're the one who said we couldn't afford that extra cost on our insurance for emergency service. So I was going to call you and tell you to come and change the tire."

Ron resisted the temptation to prove again that the extra cost for emergency service was not worth the price.

"Then I realized that I was back into my the-sky-is-falling way of thinking," she said, without giving him time to defend his financial policies. "There were panic feelings prickling at me all over. I closed my eyes, stood still, and took a deep breath. I told myself that the flat tire had nothing to do with my frustrations at work and that insurance can't solve every problem. Another deep breath. The sky had not fallen. One tire had gone flat. I tried to get the security guard to help. He told me he could help only if someone tried to steal the car. So I asked him, 'Who wants to steal a car with a flat tire?' "

"I walked to a service station and bought one of those little pressure cans filled with high-power air. I got enough air into the tire to drive back to the station and left it to be repaired."

"Good for you, honey," Ron said. "Let's eat. After dinner I'll take my car over to the station to get the tire."

"No, I made arrangements to pick it up during lunch hour tomorrow," Marsha said. "And I'm buying another of those little pressure cans to keep in the trunk. I've got this fear of the sky falling on my shoulders. Now, if you have cooked dinner as well as I have taken care of that flat tire, we're both doing great."

Prayer

Jesus, You carried the frustrations and anxieties of the world on Your shoulders. Thank You!

Homework

When you have an emotional overload, who is your best help? Suggestions: self, spouse, counselor, friends.

Intelligent people think before they speak; what they say is then more persuasive. Proverbs 16:23

* *

Do You Really Tell Your Wife Everything?

"Two weeks and two days until I get married," Tim said to his friend during coffee break. "You going to be there?"

"Wouldn't miss it for anything," Ed answered. "Are you going to be there for sure?"

"I told you that I proposed as soon as I realized I was dating above myself," Tim answered. "I just want to make sure that Jean shows up."

"Hey, man, she adores you. You know that."

"Yeah," Tim smiled, "I'm a lucky guy, and I want to keep it that way. You've been married three years, Ed. Do you really tell your wife everything you think?"

"Why do you ask that?"

"I read something that said husbands and wives shouldn't have any secrets from each other. I don't think we do, but I'm not sure."

"All of us think some pretty stupid things," Ed answered. "I don't tell my wife every thought that passes through my head. Some of them I don't even like myself."

"But how do you know what you should tell her?"

"For one thing, you've got to tell her about everything that directly affects her," Ed answered. "When we first got married, I'd make up my mind about something and then tell her. The trouble was that it sounded different when I said it aloud rather than when I just thought it. I would be sure I was right until I said it out loud; then

I wasn't so sure. That's why I learned to talk things over with Marge."

"So you do tell your wife everything, or almost everything?" Tim asked.

"I'm not so sure," Ed answered. "Some things I have to work out myself."

"What do you mean?"

"When I don't want to tell Marge something," Ed answered, "I figure there must be something wrong with my idea. If I was sure it was okay, I'd feel free to talk about it. If I don't want to talk about it, the chances are that I'm off base about something."

"So what do you do?"

"I think it over for a while by myself," Ed answered. "Or I talk to someone else like you. By the way, that's what you are doing with me now. You need to talk to Jean—but you've also got to talk to others. Test out an idea on someone else first. That may solve it. Then you don't have to make your wife a part of the problem."

"Did you know all of that when you got married?" Tim asked.

"No, and I don't know it all yet," said Ed. "But that's part of the fun of being married. Every time you get to the top of one hill, you see another. My grandfather says it stays that way for at least 53 years, and he is still learning. It's an interesting part of life."

Prayer

> Lord, help me sort out the things I think,
> So I don't have to regret the things I say.
> In Jesus' name. Amen.

Homework

Do you have someone other than your spouse whom you can talk to about your marriage?

*You are doomed! Heroes of the wine bottle! Brave and
fearless when it comes to mixing drinks! Isaiah 5:22*

A Time to Talk, a Time to Do

"Hi, honey!" Marv said as he came home via the back door on Friday evening at 6:00 p.m.

"Oh, I didn't expect you home this early," Verna answered. "The kids and I already ate dinner." The tone of both voices showed strain. Friday evenings obviously were not a good time at Marv and Verna's house.

"Okay. Let's skip that part of the conversation," he answered. "I need to talk to you."

"You may be a little too late," Verna answered.

"I hope not," Marv replied. "Something happened today that I have to tell you about."

Verna's face showed that she was afraid to take a chance on another Friday evening fight; yet she could not give up her hopes no matter how hard she tried.

"At least kiss me," Marv asked. "Then you'll know that I have not been drinking."

"Okay," she answered. "I'll take the conversation, but not the kiss." The compromise gave her a way out. She would not repeat again the usual Friday evening accusations and defenses that had become routine, but she had to do everything possible to save the marriage.

"I had a late business lunch today," Marv explained as they sat down in the living room, out of hearing range of the kids watching TV in the den.

"The other three guys were all from out of town," he continued. "One of them had heard about The Other Place and wanted to go there for lunch. That's where I generally meet the gang from my building on Friday evening. I didn't think anything about it because this was a business lunch. All work and no alcohol makes Marv a good businessman.

"We were seated at a table next to six, old, retired guys who were still there from an early lunch—and lots of drinks. The guys at my table were all our age. There was no way we could avoid listening to everything at the next table. At first I thought it was kind of fun. 'When I'm retired,' I said to myself, 'I won't have to wait until 5:00 to start the party.'

"By the time we got there they had had enough to drink to be everyone's best friend. Another round of drinks and they got into an argument about which one of them had personally won World War II. They never settled the matter, but it was clearly someone at that table.

"Another round of drinks and they decided they could sing. They started slapping the waitresses on their rears and peeking down their blouses.

"I saw myself, honey. Not myself 30 years from now, but myself on Friday night at 7:30. I need your help, Verna. Please don't let that happen to me."

"I've tried to help you, Marv," his wife answered. "But I've had to learn that I can't stop your drinking. I went to my pastor because I felt guilty. He told me I needed strength, not forgiveness. Jesus gives that too. The only thing I can do is to stop being hurt by your drinking, and keep the children from being hurt by it."

"Maybe I need both the forgiveness and the strength."

Prayer

Jesus, deliver us, and others, from all addictions. Amen.

*The one thing I do, however, is to forget what is behind
me and do my best to reach what is ahead. So I run
straight toward the goal in order to win the prize, which
is God's call through Christ Jesus to the life above.*
Philippians 3:13–14

Communication Check 3
The Rest of the Story

The longer a husband and wife are married, the more they understand each other. They learn each other's body language, the meaning of words as they use them, and what is said even in silence. Sounds great! It is, but not always.

As husbands and wives grow in their ability to communicate with one another, they also think they know what the other one will say—even before it is said. So they react not to what is being said, but what they *think* will be said. They remember when they discussed the same issue last month, or last year, and assume that their spouse will again say the same thing.

This creates a problem.

The problem is that each will react to what the other has said without waiting to hear the rest of the story. The one who started the conversation will have to defend the first statement, and the conversation never gets beyond what should have been an introduction to a discussion.

There is a solution.

When you recognize that conversation in general is going downhill in your home, or when a certain subject has blocked all other communication, call for a rest-of-the-story discussion. This is how it works.

Find at least an hour when you can be together. TV is off. Answering machine is on. Kids are in bed. Then one spouse (if necessary flip a coin to pick the lead-off talker) talks for 20 minutes without interruption. The one who is speaking must continue for the entire time, even if the last part includes childhood stories. However, the time is valuable. The one speaking has an opportunity to explain why he or she feels a certain way or does a certain thing. It gives an opportunity to present reasons as well as conclusions.

The listener will want to react to the first thing that the talker says. But that's a no-no. The listener listens, without taking notes. This allows the speaker to get past the subjects that might distract or block the conversation. The talker does not have to defend each word or statement.

By the time the first speaker has finished, the first listener will have forgotten most of the beginning of the exercise. Some of it will be unimportant. Other parts will be understood.

Then the first listener becomes the second talker, for another 20 minutes. If necessary, repeat the process with 10 minutes each on the second round.

After learning the discipline of this method, couples can do it with less structure. When each has taken time to listen as well as to speak, a good conversation can follow. Good communication is based not just on the ability to speak one's thoughts, but also on the ability to listen to the thoughts of others.

Prayer

Lord, help me hear both the words and the feelings of my spouse. In Jesus' name. Amen.

*So Jesus called a child, had him stand in front of them,
and said, "I assure you that unless you change and
become like children, you will never enter the
Kingdom of heaven." Matthew 18:2–3*

* *

I Wish I Had Known You Then

"Look what my mother sent," Kelley said as she handed Skip a large brown envelope. "It's addressed to both of us, but I think she means it for you."

Skip opened the envelope and found a stack of family pictures centered around a little girl up to about age 8.

"Are these all pictures of you?" Skip asked.

"They must be, though I can't remember all of them," Kelley answered. "I remember these when we went to Six Flags for a vacation. This is my sixth birthday—look at that hair! This is me with my cat, Fluffball."

"I wish I had known you then," Skip said.

"Would you ever have married a girl who looked like this?" Kelley asked as she held up another picture.

"But you didn't know me then either," Skip said. "You look like you were a happy little girl. I think I would have liked you."

"Were you a happy little boy?" she asked.

"Not always," he answered. "I was terribly jealous of my little brother. I used to pout about it."

"I wasn't always as happy as I look in these pictures," Kelley said. "I used to cry a lot because I was afraid of things."

"What kind of things?"

"Just things," she answered. "If I knew what kind of things they were I wouldn't have been scared of them."

"Do you still get scared about things that you don't know?"

"Sometimes. Are you still jealous of your brother?"

"No, not of my brother," Skip answered. "But I get jealous, even though I know it is silly."

"What was the happiest thing in your childhood?"

"I liked our house," he answered. "It had an upstairs and a basement. There were a lot of trees and big rooms. Sometimes I pretend I am back in that house. What was the best part of being a kid for you?"

"I liked Christmas and Thanksgiving and special family days," Kelley answered. "My family would get together for anything special like Baptisms, confirmations, weddings. We'd go to church together. Then we'd have a big dinner at our house or the home of one of my aunts and uncles. My cousins and I would explore each other's homes and get into our parents' dressers and closets."

"You know, when I look at you," Skip said, "I can still see the little girl in these pictures. And I love her too."

"I see a little boy in you lots of times," Kelley said.

"When?"

"When you forget to hang up your clothes and pretend you left them out for a reason. When you dunk your cookies in your coffee. I love that little boy too."

Prayer

Bless our memories and help us share who we were with
one another, so we may understand who we are.
In Jesus' name. Amen.

Homework

Share pictures and stories about your childhood with your spouse. Ask each other's families about your early years.

[Jesus said,] "Do for others what you want them to do for you." Matthew 7:12

* *

Whom Is the Gift For?

"Thanks for going shopping with me, Mom," Julie said. "This is fun. It's the first time I get to buy a birthday gift for a husband. You've had 29 years of experience."

"It's fun for me too," her mother replied. "And a new experience—to shop with you when we are going to use your credit card, not mine."

"Checkbook, Mom," the daughter answered. "Art and I are still operating month by month."

"Good idea. This mall has 117 stores. I hope we aren't going to all of them."

"No, I've already got this narrowed down," said Julie. "I need your help for the final choice."

"What do you have in mind?"

"I saw an ad in the paper about some new sound equipment," Julie said. "We've got a good CD player. I want to check out what I can add to it."

"I didn't know that my son-in-law liked to listen to music," Julie's mother said.

"He doesn't," Julie answered. "But I thought if I got him some extra gadgets, like earphones or a tape deck, he might get interested in using the CD."

"Is that what he wants for his birthday?"

"No," Julie said. "He's dropped a few hints about a tackle box."

"Well, then, let's go to the sports store."

"Mother! He has two tackle boxes already. He sits around sorting those fly things all the time. I want to give him something else to do—some other interest."

"Who is this gift for, you or him?" the mother asked.

"Why, him, of course. It's his birthday."

"But you are buying him what you want him to have, rather than what he'd like to have," her mother said.

"But I want to give him a gift that helps him expand his range of interests. It's for him."

"But he is already interested in fishing," the mother said. "I know you don't like fishing—just as you know that your father loves to bowl and I hate it."

"But you bought him an expensive bowling ball last Christmas."

"Sure, it was what he wanted, and I wanted to give him something that was important to him. I'm glad that he is interested in something that doesn't involve me. He needs that, and so do I. If Art likes to fish, help him enjoy it. You don't have to go along; he probably doesn't want you to. If you gave him the tackle box, you'd be showing him that you are glad he enjoys fishing."

"Oh, Mom, you're so smart!"

"No, I've just had 29 years of experience. I remember the year your father gave me a pasta maker for my birthday because he liked pasta. That's the year I explained a few things to him and learned something myself."

Prayer

Lord, help me to give to my spouse
As I would like my spouse to give to me.
In Jesus' name. Amen.

Men ought to love their wives just as they love their own bodies. A man who loves his wife loves himself.
Ephesians 5:28

The Two-Become-One Syndrome (TBOS)

In families it's sibling rivalry. In school and jobs it's competition. In clichés we say: "It's every man for himself." "It's a dog-eat-dog world out there."

We see it every day. For every winner there is a loser. It's true in sports and elections; for those who apply for jobs or make sales pitches; for those who want be on the team, the honor role, or in the class play.

Some carry the same method-of-operation into marriage. That becomes an arena with a scoreboard. Scores are posted on the I-win-you-lose principle.

This scorekeeping system in a marriage means that the two are opponents rather than partners. Problems, faults, disagreements, and failures are not owned by both but become ways for one to score points against the other. Therefore, the partners do not work together to remove the difficulty. Instead, each uses the situation to gain an advantage over the other.

I-win-you-lose methods give each spouse a way to win points by not dealing with the real issues:

• Get angry. Anger changes the subject. It makes my feelings more important than your facts. It hides the problem because we have to deal with the anger.

• Don't talk. As long as one won't talk about a subject, neither can deal with it. One way not to lose a war is not to fight. If I won't talk about it, I decide that I am right and don't have to talk about the issues. As long as I don't tell you why I am right, you can't tell me why I am wrong.

• Talk too much. As long as I am talking, I don't have to listen to you. The more I talk, the more right I sound; so I win on points.

• Be too busy. The wage-earner's excuse: "Look, I work my buns off to pay for things that this family wants." The homemaker's excuse: "I never get a day off. There's no vacation or coffee break on my job."

One spouse wins and the other loses, but the marriage always loses. Marriage is based on a two-become-one-syndrome (TBOS). It not only puts two people in the same bed and on the same checking account; it puts two people into one being. Their bodies, minds, and spirits connect. What hurts one hurts both. What gives joy to one gives joy to both. If one hurts the other, he/she also hurts himself/herself. If one gives pleasure to the other, he/she also receives pleasure.

The TBOS is not created by a marriage ceremony or a wedding license. Sharing sex, breakfast, and credit cards will not cause TBOS. But it all helps. Two lives become one when each spouse is committed to the well-being of the other. One can never be happy at the expense of the other. One cannot be happy without the other sharing the experience.

The Bible uses TBOS to explain the relationship of Christ and the church. It is a relationship of love, given and received by both. The relationship of Christ and the church is more than an example for the relationship of husband and wife. It is Christ's love for both the man and the woman that helps make them husband and wife. TBOS is a gift from God.

Prayer

Jesus, help the two of us live as one. Amen.

*I waited patiently for the Lord's help; then He listened to
me and heard my cry. Psalm 40:1*

●●●●●●●●●●●●●●●●●●●●●●●●●●●●●●

I Need to Look at My Thoughts

"Hi, Jill," Rob said as he recognized his sister's voice
on the phone. "How's my favorite niece and nephew?"

"Your only niece and nephew are fine," Jill answered.
"Your sister is a candidate for nuthood. Being a single
parent has its bad years."

"Sorry, Sis," he answered. "I'm glad you called. What
can I do?"

"I really don't need you to do anything—except listen," she answered. "And so you know, there is no major
crisis. I have to make a lot of decisions for the kids every
week, and I can't talk to their father."

"Isn't he keeping in touch with the kids?"

"Oh, he calls them every week and I talk to him too,"
she answered. "But if we had been able to talk about
things when we were married, we wouldn't be divorced
now. So I avoid anything that might be a problem. I know
it sounds strange to say this, but I miss talking to him."

"I thought he never talked," Rob said.

"He didn't," she answered, "but I did. I realize that he
never heard a word I said, but at least I could talk without
having to face the fact that I was talking to myself. I've
discovered something—that's why I called you."

"And what is your discovery?"

"I can have an idea that makes good sense when I
think about it. I mull it over, think of all the pros and
cons, and decide what to do. I'm sure that I'm right until I
put it into action. An idea that made good sense inside

my head can be real dumb when I throw it out in the public arena."

"This explains why you miss your ex-husband?" Rob asked.

"Yes. Even though he rarely helped with the children, I would talk to him about everything. Because I had a reason to get my thoughts out of my head, I could see them in a different way. I didn't need him to give me a different point of view; I just need to see my own ideas from a different point of view."

"Have you tried telling your dog all of this?" Rob asked.

"No, I called you because you won't put your paws on me when I talk to you," she answered. "Are you taking this seriously?"

"Yes, I understand," Rob said. "I am glad you called because I think about you and the kids often. We always include you in our bedtime prayers."

"I don't need you to tell me what I should do," Jill said. "But I need you to listen and see if I make sense."

"Okay."

"I hope you are sitting down; I've got a long list. I need to talk about Cindy's report card and what to do about Matt's total lack of interest in school. I also want to talk about the best way to plan a vacation that includes both sets of grandparents and what to do when . . . "

Prayer

Holy Spirit, help us know when we need to listen to one another and when we need to speak to one another.
In Jesus' name. Amen.

Homework

Listen.

Each of you men should know how to live with his wife
in a holy and honorable way, not with a lustful desire,
like the heathen who do not know God.
1 Thessalonians 4:4–5

Sex and Antisex 1

The best stories about sex are not written in a book; shown in a movie, on a stage, on TV; or captured in a picture. The great love stories of literature and drama are tragedies. Happy sex stories make poor public entertainment—but great lives. Real sex is private, between one man and one woman. Adding a reporter, storyteller, or photographer changes sex to voyeurism.

Attempts to record the sexual relationship changes sex to antisex—not nonsex as in celibacy or abstention, but antisex as in being against the true purpose of sexuality.

In the animal world, sex is useful only for procreation. Males and females in the pasture and zoo show no sexual interest in each other except during the rutting season when conception occurs. But in the human world, sex is more than a way to produce more human beings. Sex is, first of all, a way to produce the relationship of a husband and wife who love one another so they can become parents who share their love with a child.

Sex creates a relationship between a man and woman that makes them become one. Antisex divides. When people seek multiple sex partners they are avoiding the unity that monogamy creates. In such cases the sexual act is the goal. That is antisex. In sex, the sexual act is the means to achieving the goal of a lifelong union between one man and one woman.

Sex is a way to make love. Love creates the need for sex, and sex results in an increased love. If you make cookies, you have cookies available. If you make money, you have money to save and invest. If you make love, you have love to enjoy together and to reinvest in each other.

Antisex is a way to make hate. Think of all the dirty words that are used to refer to sexual intercourse. They express hate or violence. Such words are used not only to destroy the self-esteem of others, but also to damage the one who speaks them.

God created sex to bond two people together. Antisex is created by sin. It is no wonder that Satan attacks human sexuality. It is a precious gift from God. Sexuality involves an exclusive love—a husband and a wife love each other in a way that they love no one else. Through Christ, God has also given us an *inclusive* love. The love between God and us is not a mutual attraction like that of a husband and wife. Rather, God gives His love to all, without limitations.

Human love, even that between a husband and a wife, will fall short. At times it will not function. But the love of Christ is always there. Jesus comes into a marriage, not as a third party, but as one who loves both spouses and gives them His love so they can share it with one another. His love changes antisex back to sex.

Prayer

Thank You, God,
For giving to me the gift of sex to give to my spouse
And to my spouse to give to me.
In Jesus' name. Amen.

Since you are God's people, it is not right that any matters of sexual immorality or indecency or greed should even be mentioned among you. Ephesians 5:3

* *

Sex and Antisex 2

Since true sexuality cannot be recorded by cameras or the printed page, and since sex is a natural and important part of life, it is often presented as antisex.

Sometimes people talk or write about sex as though it were humorous. Some of the funniest plays, books, and stories are about sex. True sex is fun; it is not funny. We need to make it funny because we have to talk about it, we need to learn about it, and we need to know that others feel about it as we do.

Humor is a safe way to work sex into a conversation. When a subject is too personal, we joke to break the tension. But that's the problem. The humor blocks the road to the deeper intimacy that sex offers. It turns to antisex.

Sometimes sex is presented as dirty. Something becomes dirty when its use is perverted. When money controls others or buys status, the money is dirty. When religion is used to serve self rather than God, it is dirty. When sex is used to degrade the body, to take rather than to give, to divide rather than unite, it is dirty. When sex is physical only, it is dirty. When the use of sex destroys other relationships and hurts other people, it is dirty.

Sex is a beautiful gift from God. It is a way God gave a man and a woman to give themselves totally to each other and to share in His act of creation. To get us away from God, Satan separates us from one another. If he can makes us change sex to antisex, he has destroyed one of the most lasting bonds that can exist for human beings. Christ came to restore all the unity that God wants His people to have—including the sexual union. His grace and forgiveness change antisex back to sex.

Sex is sometimes presented as violence. Rape and molestation are called sexual crimes. They are not sexual, but antisexual. They are an expression of hatred for others or for self.

When we see sex as violence we are afraid to take the risk of being vulnerable in sex. Those who have been sexually molested or raped have been hurt by the violence of sex. Those who have learned about sex through the violence of TV and movies or physical abuse between parents can be afraid of the closeness of loving sex.

Sometimes sex is presented as boring. Sex education can be misunderstood as an academic subject. Teaching sex as an organ recital by learning the proper names for body parts is necessary; but that is anatomy, not sexuality. Some sex education courses try to desensitize sexuality by removing the mystery and privacy of sex. Yet it is that very personal and intimate expression of sex that makes it the bonding and lasting relationship between a man and a woman.

Sex education is needed. Each person needs to know the names and functions of the body parts. All people need to know the details of conception. But much more is needed. Sex is beautiful because it brings together the totality of two people into one relationship. Sex is a physical, mental, emotional, and spiritual experience. To participate in sex is to give oneself totally to another and to totally accept the other person.

Prayer

God, bless our sexual union. In Jesus' name. Amen.

Correct someone, and afterward he will appreciate it
more than flattery. Proverbs 28:23

Proverbs for the Refrigerator Door

1. If you give me a choice, then accept my decision and don't tell me what you would have done.

2. It's okay for me to find fault with my side of the family. But they are mine; so you keep out of it.

3. If you ask me to help or I volunteer, that means it's your job and I am helping you. So we'll do it your way. But if it is *our* job, we'll do it our way.

4. I don't have to have as much energy as you, and I am not a wimp because of it.

5. Don't be surprised to find, when you hear me talking to others, that I am well-informed, have good opinions, and can express them.

6. I am flattered when others notice that you are attractive because it shows what good taste I have.

7. If you ever think of being unfaithful to me, that will be your problem, because you will lose the best thing you've got going for you.

8. The father is persistent. The mother is consistent. The children are stubborn.

9. Becoming parents is the greatest challenge young adults can have to their values, beliefs, and goals in life. Will they be willing to teach their children to live by their own patterns?

10. The best reality therapy for people around 40 who think that at last they are in control of their lives is teenage children.

11. Grandparents do not spoil grandchildren. Grandchildren spoil grandparents.

12. The best heart medicine for a sixty-year-old is a two-year-old grandchild.

13. Conversation in a marriage in trouble:
"What's the matter, dear?"
"You ought to know."

14. It is an example of sexual luxury to be occasionally able to have routine, even so-so, sex.

15. If a man and woman must live together before marriage to find out if their relationship will work, they will have to wait for at least 50 years before they are sure.

16. Don't wait to get married or to have children until you can afford it. Some things cannot be paid for with money.

17. On your honeymoon, remember what your third-grade math teacher taught you: "We're going to do this over and over until we get it right."

18. A prayer before you share a meal together:
"Come, Lord Jesus, be our guest,
and let this food to us be blessed. Amen."
And then expect Him to be there.

Prayer

*Lord, make us secure enough to speak to one another
and wise enough to listen to one another.
In Jesus' name. Amen.*

Homework

Search the book of Proverbs in the Bible for words of wisdom that are needed in your marriage. Watch for other proverbs in your daily lives. Copy proverbs for yourself and your spouse and post them on the refrigerator.

*Then the Lord God said, "It is not good for the man
to live alone. I will make a suitable companion
to help him." Genesis 2:18*

A Velcro Marriage

It may not be good for a man, or a woman, to live alone, but sometimes it is also not good for a man and a woman to be together. Some husbands and wives find their greatest joy in their marriage relationship. Others find their greatest misery in theirs. What makes the difference? What choices do a husband and wife have?

One important difference is the way two people relate to each other. They can have different images of what a husband and a wife are.

Some couples look good together. They look like Ken and Barbie dolls or the bride and groom on the top of a wedding cake. If their unity is established by appearance, the two have become a set, rather than one. They are like salt and pepper shakers that look good together but are not united.

Other couples become one by becoming one or the other. One is the coffee, the other the cream. They are poured together and become one, but people drink coffee, not cream. So also in marriage, sometimes one is consumed by the other. That one loses his/her identity at the expense of both.

Another image: Two pieces of Velcro become one. They are attached to one another, and each piece holds tightly to the other. Though they become one, they can still be divided. As the two pieces of Velcro are pulled apart, one can hear the sound of tearing. That ripping sound also occurs in marriage. When tensions occur, the husband and wife pull apart—and they feel the pain of their separation.

But they also know they have the ability to be reunited again. Velcro is made so it can be pulled apart without destroying either piece. The two pieces can become one again. A healthy marriage needs two independent members who can both become dependent. When they are united they become one, but each remains an individual. Stresses and strains may pull them apart. They will feel the pain. However, they also know they have the ability to reknit.

In a Christian marriage Jesus offers the way to bring and hold spouses together—not by the legal force of a marriage license nor by guilt about broken wedding vows, but by a renewable love that brings a fresh union every day. Christ forgives the wrongs that pull husbands and wives apart. Even in their times of tension, He gives them love that helps them face their problems with the assurance that their marriage need not be destroyed.

Prayer

Thank You, God, for the times
When we are one with no divisions.
Help us when we feel pulled apart
So we can become one again.
In Jesus' name. Amen.

Homework

Identify the tensions and stresses that pull you and your spouse apart. What methods and assurances do you have that help you be united again?

Love does not keep a record of wrongs.
1 Corinthians 13:5

He Had to Be Angry to Tell Me

"We've been married for 22 years, and for the first time in a long time I'm worried about our marriage. Maybe that's the problem. I've lost something that was so important to me.

"We had an argument Saturday morning. I know this sounds silly, but I can't even remember what it was about. One of the good things about our marriage is that we can have disagreements and tell each other. Just because I have forgotten what our argument was about does not mean that it was not important. We were both angry, and we both said so. I didn't worry about it. Maybe that's why I forgot what it was about. I don't mind being angry at my husband because I can tell him—at least I thought I could. And I don't mind having him angry at me because I always thought he would tell me.

"Then after we had finished the argument—at least we both had said what we needed to say—he added something. Right out of the blue—it had nothing to do with what we had been talking about—he just said, 'And furthermore, I don't like the way you iron my shirts.'

"You know my husband is in the military. Has been for all of our married life. I thought it looked nice to iron creases down the front of his shirts—one on each side right over the pockets. It was a lot of extra work, but I learned how to do it when we were first married—you know, you want to do special things then. I noticed that most of the other guys in his outfit didn't have the

117

creases in their shirts. But I thought that made my husband look special. And even though I quit doing some dumb things like ironing underwear and pillowcases, I kept on ironing the creases in his shirts.

"Now he tells me that he doesn't like it. And he had to be angry to tell me. Twenty years ago he should have said, 'Honey, don't bother putting the creases in my shirts.' But he didn't! Instead, he must have felt some kind of resentment every time he put on one of those shirts. Now he tells me! And he had to be angry to say it.

"That's what bothers me. Do I do other things that irk him? Is he upset at the way I laugh? or the way I entertain guests? or the way I eat? I don't know anymore. I feel insecure. I don't mind having him disagree with something I say or be upset at something I do. There's a lot of things about him that tick me off too. But I tell him.

"And I always thought he was honest with me. But now I'm not sure. Thanks for listening to me. I know what I've got to do. I've got to ask him. I'd rather risk hearing a lot of bad things that he is really thinking, than for me to worry about everything I say or do."

Prayer

Jesus,
Open our ears to hear each other,
Our mouths to speak to one another,
And in that order. Amen.

Homework

Can you criticize your spouse in a constructive way without being angry? Can your spouse do the same with you?

[Jesus said,] "The measure you use for others is the one that God will use for you." Luke 6:38

On a Bad Day

She puts labels on things. When we were first married I was afraid to sit still because I thought I'd end up with a sign, HUSBAND, on my forehead.

He leaves the cap off the toothpaste.

She collects empty boxes—then she has to go find a big box to keep her other boxes in.

He turns on the TV in one room while the radio is playing in another—a cacophony attacking me.

When we come home she has to go around and touch everything in the house to see if it is still there.

He pulls off his socks and leaves them like little tennis balls in the laundry. It takes two days for them to dry.

She wears socks to bed, in July, in Tucson, Arizona.

He spends $35.00 on stuff to raise two dollars worth of vegetables that don't taste very good anyway.

She makes sympathetic and disapproving sounds as she watches TV.

He reads magazines backwards.

She says "borrow" when she means "loan."

He leaves a trail of paper napkins with the four corners rolled into paper spikes—then he tweedles them in his ears.

She uses plastic cups, forks, and spoons to make entertaining easier; then she washes them to use the next time.

He eagerly waits for the mail, opens it as he walks through the house, and lets it fall where it may.

She writes checks without listing them in the checkbook.

He writes checks without listing them in the checkbook.

She asks me the same questions three times because she does not listen to my answer.

He parks the car so I can't get in and out easily—even though I've asked him not to many times.

She wants to be five minutes late when we are to be guests at someone else's home.

He wants to be five minutes early when we are to be guests at someone else's home.

She eats lettuce sandwiches.

He puts mustard and jelly on the same sandwich.

I put up with her garbage because I love her.

I put up with his garbage because I love him.

Authors' note: We each agreed that we would not put anything on this list without the other's approval. We would not hurt each other by things that should be private. But we want readers to know the list has been censored.

Prayer

Lord Jesus,
As you love us while we are still sinners,
So help us to love one another even when we fail.
In Jesus' name. Amen.

Homework

Can you accept the fact that your spouse finds fault with you? Can you tell your spouse what faults you see in him/her?

Love is patient and kind; it is not jealous or conceited or proud. 1 Corinthians 13:4

On a Good Day

She touches me.

He surprises me by asking what we were doing 19, or 25, or 39 years ago on that date. Then he tells me what we had for dinner (and that he was plotting to propose marriage) or that we were on vacation and a bird spattered me.

She asks me for an explanation if she thinks I've done or said something unkind.

He helps me understand investments and keeps me up to date on our finances.

She cares how she looks when I'm the only one around.

He always hangs up his pants and coats; I've heard reports about other husbands.

She fixes special meals, just for me.

He shares the good things I can do with others.

She has taught me to enjoy art.

He can find his way around any city or country, walking, driving, or on public transportation systems.

She encouraged me to live out my dream of being a writer, even when it meant that I took working vacations away from the family.

We've moved 12 times, and he knows what kind of house I like and that I feel better if there are big trees in the yard.

She lived through years of near poverty with me and never complained.

He knows the kind of clothing and jewelry that please me.

When I look at her now I can still see the same person I first saw 40 years ago.

He holds my hand as we fall asleep.

She is a good mother to our children.

Authors' note: Again, this is a censored list. This time we did not list the things that belong only to us. To share them would take something away from their value.

Prayer

Thank You, Lord God,
For the gift that you gave
And keep on giving
In our relationship with one another.
In Jesus' name. Amen.

Homework:

If fault-finding and lack of compliments are a problem in your relationship:

• Give each partner five red buttons and five blue ones.

• When one finds fault with another, he/she puts a red button in a cup.

• When one compliments the other, he/she puts a blue button in the cup.

• If one runs out of red buttons first, he/she is not allowed to find a fault until all his/her blue buttons are used.

• If one runs out of blue buttons first, he/she gets to decide what they watch on TV that weekend.

• Repeat as often as necessary.

[Jesus said,] "Do not judge others, so that God will not judge you, for God will judge you in the same way you judge others, and He will apply to you the same rules you apply to others." Matthew 7:1–2

Don't Let 10 Percent Bad Ruin 90 Percent Good

"Come on, Pete," Adam said. "Tradition says I should take you out for a drink—and, you know, for a man-to-man talk." The rehearsal dinner was over. Pete wanted to be with his brother, who was also his best man, but the wedding activities had kept them busy.

"I'm too excited for a drink tonight," Pete answered. "But I think tradition also says you should give me some advice. Let's take a walk."

The two brothers walked out into the cool night air. They had spent little time alone together since Adam got married four years ago.

"Okay, tell me," Pete asked, "how do I have a perfect marriage?"

"You can't, because you're a part of it—remember, this is your big brother you're talking to."

"So you know a few things that no one else does," Pete answered. "Becky thinks she's getting the best."

"And she is," the older brother answered, "but the best is not perfect. Maybe you need to be reminded that Becky can't be a perfect wife either."

"But it seems like she will be," Pete answered. "That's why I want to be the best husband possible. She deserves it."

"When Jan and I got married," Adam said, "the pastor told us not to let 10 percent bad destroy 90 percent good. That's helped us. Trying to be perfect can drive you nuts. If you do that, one little thing can cause you to lose the whole marriage. If you accept the fact that you are going to goof up now and then, you will also understand that your wife will make mistakes too."

"But Becky and I want our marriage to work," Pete said. "Do you realize that half of the people in our wedding party have been divorced? We talked about it the other night, and it scares us."

"Hey, I hear you, little brother," Adam said, "and I'm on your side. I just don't want you to think that one problem will blow your marriage out of the water. Becky's a great gal, but she can't be perfect. And you shouldn't expect her to be. You shouldn't try to pretend you're going to be the best husband in the world either. Let her see where you hurt. Ask her for help when you can't be the kind of husband you want to be. *Perfection causes competition.* When you let her see your weak spots, and you are willing to see that she can be vulnerable too, then you'll know you need each other and be glad about it."

The two brothers walked on in silence for a while.

"It's easy for me to say that you're the best brother that I've got," Pete said, "because you're the only one. And I'm only going to have one wife too—for the rest of my life. So she'll be the best."

"Sounds good to me," Adam answered.

Prayer
> Lord Jesus, help us forgive each other as you have
> forgiven us. Amen.

Homework
Are you, or is your spouse, a perfectionist? Do you expect perfection from each other? Talk about it.

*I pray that your love will keep on growing more and
more, together with true knowledge and perfect
judgment. Philippians 1:9*

● ●

Communication Check 4
Can You Say What I Said?

Part of your wedding may have included a repeat-af-ter-me part. It's easy to repeat the exact words that others have spoken. But it can also be dangerous, because you may be saying something that you do not understand.

It's more difficult to repeat, in your own words, what someone else has said, in a way that the other person will agree with. Try it with your spouse.

First, think about times when you have had diffi-culties in communication. Do you often misquote one another? Did one say, "We don't have any money for va-cation this year" and the other tell the family, "He/she said we can't keep the cable TV"?

Did she say, "That shirt doesn't look good with those trousers," then he told his brother, "She always com-plains about how I dress"?

Did he say, "I don't like spinach," then she told her friends, "He won't eat any fresh vegetables"?

One said, "I think we have some problems in our marriage that we should talk about." The other said, "He/she wants a divorce."

One said, "I'd like to go to church and be active in the congregation." The other said, "He/she thinks we have to spend all our time at church and give all our money to the church."

Often we misunderstand what our marriage partner

says because we either exaggerate or minimize the other's words.

Next step: Can you state your spouse's opinion on religion, politics, finances, discipline of children, relationship with in-laws, etc.? Try it, and see if your spouse agrees with what you think he/she believes. Try it first on safe subjects. In some families, religion, politics, and social issues are safe topics; in others they are not.

One partner should state an opinion. Then the other repeats back in different words what the first said. This exercise requires the speaker to be clear in stating an opinion, and it requires the listener to pay attention. Both qualities are needed in good communication.

Next, try the same method on some topics that you might not have talked about. Some husbands and wives have been married for years and can talk about necessary things but have avoided certain subjects. Talk to each other about opinions on God, death, funerals, living wills, retirement, fantasies. Do this for two reasons. First, learn how to give your opinion and to listen to your spouse's view so you can repeat it. But also do it to share with one another what you think about important subjects.

Finally, remember subjects that have caused conflicts in the past. Discuss them by trading roles. You say what you believe your spouse thinks on the subject, and let your spouse give your views. As you do this you may realize that your spouse doesn't understand you, and you may also have not listened to the other's views. Then work on it!

Prayer
Thank You, God, for giving me two ears for hearing and one mouth for talking. In Jesus' name. Amen.

What you should say is this: "If the Lord is willing, we will live and do this or that." James 4:15

The Nominations Are . . .

Ted and Patty were eating dinner at home—with a lot of silence.

"I guess we've pretty well ruined Memorial Day weekend already," he finally said, "haven't we?"

"I guess so, and it's still two weeks away."

The night before, Ted had come home and told her about his plans for them to spend the weekend with some friends who were going camping. Patty said she had already told her parents that they would spend the weekend with them. Each expected the other to change the plans already made. They talked about it a long time but went to bed without resolving the problem.

"I've thought about this all day," Ted said, "and I can't figure a way out. I felt like coming home and telling you that I had canceled out on the camping trip and that we would go visit your parents. But I know you'd feel bad all weekend."

"And I almost called my mother to tell her we wouldn't be there. But I doubt if you'd have much fun on a camping trip with me now. Maybe we should each do what we planned for ourselves."

"No," he said. "This is our first weekend holiday since we've been married. I want to be with you."

"I want to be with you too," she said. "But where?"

"I suppose we could just stay at home together," he said. "I'd like to be with you—and we'd save some money."

"That might solve it this time," she said, "but how do we handle other decisions? We've both managed our own lives for so long, it's hard to have to do it for two."

"I took a walk during lunch time," he said, "and I remembered how my parents used to handle this kind of thing."

"Dad would say, 'We've got a long weekend coming up. What are we going to do?' Mom would say, 'I nominate a camping trip.' Dad would add, 'I nominate a visit to my parents.' Then they would add some more. We kids had to sit at the table while they talked about all the nominations."

"But when they finally reached a decision, it was made by both of them. No one won. And no one lost. We made our mistake because we each decided what we wanted to do—and expected the other one to do it."

"I heard your parents talking about nominations one time, and I didn't have a clue to what they were talking about," said Patty. "Now I understand. It seems to work very well for them."

"Grandma told me that the nominations for my name included Clarence, Fremont, and Orville—all names of my great-uncles," Ted said. "Thank God for Great-Uncle Theodore!"

Prayer

Lord,
When we find ourselves on two different roads,
Show us a way to merge the traffic.
In Jesus' name. Amen.

Homework

Check the way you and your spouse make decisions. Do you expect your spouse to agree with your decision, or do you reach the decision together?

*Do not conform yourselves to the standards of this world,
but let God transform you inwardly by a complete
change of your mind. Romans 12:2*

Rerun? Or Renew?

Jake walked into the cantina. It was Friday, 6:00 p.m. Happy hour was under way. He had not been there for almost 13 years—since he started dating Sara—but everything seemed to be the same. He walked by the half-empty tables and friendly greetings to stand at the bar. He was there as an observer, not a participant.

He looked around the room. There was less smoke than he had remembered. The music was different but played at the same blaring volume. Though he didn't recognize a single face, they all looked familiar. It was a happy party.

Then Jake turned his attention to individuals. First he looked for the 25-year-olds—himself 13 years ago. There were fewer than he remembered. They were the true singles—the never-been-married, a minority at a singles bar.

Jake watched them closely. They were having a good time. They had worked five days with TGIF in mind. Now it was time to live it up. To understand their happiness Jake had to turn his mind back. He had to forget what it was like to share life with a wife, to want to be home rather than in a crowd, to want to be with one person rather than many. He had to forget the miracle of seeing his children born, the wet, sloppy kisses and hugs from them when he came home. If these people knew about such things, they were looking forward to them, not thinking of what they had lost.

Then his eyes looked at others, a man his age with tight pants and shirt opened to the navel, the woman (still with a cigarette) laughing like a teenager and shaped like a grandmother. He saw costumes instead of clothing. He saw people playing old tapes.

Jake remembered the hours that he and Sara had spent with the counselor. At first he enjoyed it. The counselor would smile and listen. He and Sara could talk without arguing in the presence of this pleasant stranger. The counselor was married. Jake was sure he would understand the problem and help Sara see reality.

One day the counselor asked to see Jake alone. No longer just a listener, the counselor gave him a clear opinion. He gave Jake a choice: Either change or get a divorce. He told Jake that he had given only half of himself to his wife and children. The other half had remained single, living his own life. Jake had protested. He wanted the marriage. He loved his family. The counselor agreed but told him he had put limits on the love. He wanted his own life and theirs too. He couldn't have both. He had to make the choice.

Jake looked at the one empty chair at a table. He knew he could go sit in that chair. He thought of the kitchen table at home. It also had one empty chair. He knew he could go sit in that chair. But he couldn't sit in both.

Prayer

Lord God, help me understand today's problems,
By remembering what has happened in the past,
And by knowing that what I do today
Will change tomorrow.
In Jesus' name. Amen.

*Thoughtless words can wound as deeply as any sword,
but wisely spoken words can heal. Proverbs 12:18*

• •

What Are Your Words Worth?

Words are like checks. One may write a check for a few dollars, or for thousands of dollars. The value of the check is determined by the person who writes it.

It's the same way with words. One may use a word at one time and give it a certain value. At another time the same person may speak or write the same word and give it a much different value. This is how it works:

I may say, "I want . . . " The word *want* could have a value of 50 cents—just a passing fancy or a slight itch for something. Or the same word, pronounced with the same tone of voice, could be a 50-dollar word. It could be my deepest desire, my most urgent need.

Or I may say, "I believe . . . " That word could be a 50-cent word expressing my opinion about tomorrow's weather—and I'm no expert on forecasting weather. Or it could be my response to God's grace through Jesus Christ—a 50,000-dollar word.

When words are passed back and forth between speakers and hearers, between writers and readers, both parties must know the value of the words. A husband may say, "I'd like to take up tennis." He may have meant it as a 50-cent word. He said it because he thought he needed some exercise and the other guys at work play tennis. But his wife heard it as a 50-dollar word. She takes money out of other parts of the budget, which are already operating in the red, to buy tennis equipment for her spouse. She sacrificed a lot to buy something for him that he really didn't want, all because they didn't understand the value of words.

A wife may say, "You're losing a little of your hair in the back of your head." The husband may hear it as a 50-dollar remark. Does his wife think he looks old? Should he buy a toupee? Or have a hair transplant? After a week of worry, he asks his wife what he should do about his bald spot. But she doesn't know what he is talking about. She had made a 50-cent remark. She had no worries about his slight loss of hair.

Both the speaker and the listener, the writer and the reader, must establish the value of words. You don't write a check without filling in the amount; so don't speak or write without knowing the value of your words. You don't accept a check without knowing what it is worth; so don't listen to or read words without knowing their value.

As a husband and wife grow in their ability to communicate, they establish a par value for words. In normal conversation all words are worth 10 bucks. The one who speaks needs to let the other know when words have a greater or lesser value. The one who hears needs to verify if he/she thinks the value of a word is higher or lower than usual.

Words work—when we know how to use them.

Prayer

Holy Spirit,
Open my ears to hear words
As gifts from others to me,
And open my mouth to speak words
As gifts to others.
In Jesus' name. Amen.

[Jesus] said to them, "A man who divorces his wife and marries another woman commits adultery against his wife. In the same way, a woman who divorces her husband and marries another man commits adultery." Mark 10:11–12

The Next Time Around

Barney and Ned struggled against the flow of the crowd as they headed toward their seats at a basketball game.

"Hey, Barney," called a man.

"Hi, Al," Barney answered. "Long time, no see."

"Yeah, been busy," Al said. "My wife said we are invited to your wedding—at a church yet."

"Yes, I hope you can come."

"Sorry," Al answered, "got plans for that weekend. But I'll catch you next time around."

"So who's your friend?" Ned asked later.

"Not really a friend," Barney replied. "We grew up next door to each other, and he still lives in the same house by my parents."

"Sorry about his nasty remark," Ned said.

"Thanks, but I can handle it now. I don't hide from the fact that I've been married twice before."

"I didn't know you then," Ned said. "But I think you and Jeannie have a great thing going. Don't let jerks like that put a trip on you."

"I put the trip on myself," Barney replied. "When you are a two-time loser, you have to think about it."

"You were 20 when you married for the first time. The next was a rebound. You can't hold that against yourself."

"I don't," Barney answered, "but not for the reasons you might think. Jeannie's pastor required us to go through premarital counseling. We talked about these things. I know you go to church, Ned, and you are used to this religion talk. It's a part of Jeannie's life too. And I want it to be a part of mine."

"Good."

"I thought the pastor was going to talk about an annulment as the way around my first two marriages. But he didn't take that way out. And he didn't tell me that divorce is normal for people who get married young or on the rebound—like the counselor that I went to after my second."

"What did he say?" Ned asked.

"He said that divorce is sin," Barney replied. "At first that threw me for a loop. But Jeannie understood and explained it to me. This Jesus of theirs said that if you get a divorce and marry someone else it is a sin. That's what I did the first time. I jumped from one wife to the other."

"And this time?" Ned asked.

"I was married and I got divorced. Then, this is where Jesus comes in. He forgives me. That's His thing, they say. So instead of being a divorced person, I'm single again. And I didn't have to find an excuse for myself. I can see I was wrong in the ways I got married before. And I was wrong in those marriages too. But I'm forgiven. I've got a clean slate. That's what Jeannie and her pastor believe. I'm starting to believe it too."

Prayer Suggestion

Pray for those who have been divorced. Ask God to help them deal with all problems from previous marriages before they enter new relationships.

[Jesus said,] "For your heart will always be where your riches are." Matthew 6:21

Our Hope Chest

"What's this?" Debi asked as she pulled a small wooden box from a packing crate. She was helping her friend Louise unpack. Louise's husband, Bob, was still in the military and wouldn't be home for another month.

"That's our hope chest," Louise answered.

"Look, I knew you all through high school, and you certainly didn't have a hope chest," Debi said. "And the Bob I know wouldn't have a clue about owning one."

"At least I knew about hope chests because my grandmother told me," Louise said. "My mother gave me this. Some furniture company gave one to all the girls in her high school class. They hoped all the girls would buy a real hope chest. Open it. It's really made of cedar."

"It smells good," Debi said. She noticed that it was filled with small pieces of paper. "But this looks like it might be private stuff," she added as she closed the lid and passed it back to her friend.

"It is personal, but I can tell you about it," Louise said. "After Bob and I were married for about six months we realized how different we are. Our families sort of look and sound like each other, but we have major differences. We had a hard time understanding each other.

"So we decided that our differences were things we brought into our marriage—like the things brides used to put in hope chests. Only instead of seeing our differences as problems, we decided they were good things that we would give to each other."

"Maybe I should use this idea," Debi said. "Al's family is weird compared to mine. And he thinks mine is strange."

"It has helped us," Louise said. "We each wrote out our special gifts to the other on pieces of paper. Bob's family lived in one house all of his childhood. He knows every relative he ever had, down to the third cousins twice removed. That's part of the reason we're moving back here. At first I resented all of his family, but he gave them to me as a gift.

"And I had something to give him. My family moved around a lot before they settled here. I went to seven different grade schools. I thought that was bad, until Bob and I had to move around because of the military. I discovered I had something to give him, because I knew how to go out and make friends—and find stores.

"His family reads lots of magazines and books. He knows a lot about history and people. He's given that to me. I enjoyed music as a kid, and he's tone deaf. But I've helped him appreciate good music. He likes to go to concerts with me now. We both grew up going to church, but he has given me a deeper understanding of our faith."

"Sounds like you two have it all worked out," Debi said. "Maybe Bob should have a talk with Al before we get married."

"We'll be glad to show you our hope chest and let you smell the cedar," Louise said. "But you'll have to find your own gifts to each other. These belong to us."

Prayer

Lord, help us see our differences as gifts that we can share with one another. In Jesus' name. Amen.

*Be on your guard, then, so that you will not lose what
we have worked for, but will receive your reward in full.*
2 John 8

A Picture-Perfect Family

"There's a letter from my Aunt Clara on the table,"
Rita called to her husband. "You had better read it."

"Your aunt who lives in Germany?" Tony responded.
"I haven't even met her."

"I know, but read the last paragraph."

Tony scanned the letter. It was typical of his wife's
extended family. Details about relatives he hardly knew.
Aunt Clara was simply delighted that her sister, Rita's
mother, had been with her for a week. Then he came to
the last paragraph:

> Your mother showed me your family
> picture. What a *beautiful* family!! Little Joey
> looks just like your Uncle Ed. And you and
> Tony are so *radiant*! I can see how much
> you are in love. You are a picture-perfect
> family.

Tony sat down, tears running down his cheeks.

"Do you remember the day we had that picture
taken?" Rita asked.

"Yes. We hadn't talked to each other for three days."

"Yet we are a picture-perfect family," she said. "Do
you know that all of our friends and family are going to
be shocked when they hear we are getting a divorce?"

"You make it sound final," he said. "We haven't decided that yet."

"You are the one who called the lawyer," she said.

"Looked up a number," he corrected. "I haven't called yet."

"Why not?"

"Because divorce doesn't fit my self-image," he said. "And it doesn't fit into my picture of you and Joey either."

"That's the problem in our marriage. The video is great, the audio is lousy."

"We've spent almost five years trying to look and act like we think we should be," Tony said. "We've fooled everyone—maybe even ourselves. I've always tried to be what other people wanted me to be. You have too. And it hasn't worked."

"We could blame it on our parents," she said. "Both sets expected a lot from us. But we're adults. We've got to accept the responsibility for who we are."

"What do you want out of me?" Tony asked.

"I honestly don't know anymore," Rita answered. "And I don't know what I can give you as a wife."

"Does that mean I should call the lawyer?" he asked.

"If we have to keep on pretending that we are a perfect couple and perfect parents, yes, call the lawyer."

"Is there another choice?"

"We could call a marriage counselor. But that means we don't take the picture of us to impress the counselor like we have done before. We have to go as we are."

"Do you know whom to call?"

"We could start by calling our pastor. He may know where to send us."

Prayer

Dear Jesus, help us keep our lives in focus so we can see what we are, not what we pretend to be. Amen.

*In the same way the Spirit also comes to help us, weak as
we are. For we do not know how we ought to pray; the
Spirit Himself pleads with God for us in groans that
words cannot express. Romans 8:26*

* *

Who Made the Decision?

Zack stood at the street corner. Turn left, half a
block, and he would be home—where his wife was angry
with him. Turn right for more time to think. He turned
right.

What had gone wrong? Once again he retraced the
events that led to the anger exchanged an hour ago. It
had started four months ago. He had gotten a call from
out of the blue with the hint of a job offer—six states
away. He knew Janet would not be excited about moving
again. They had made friends here. She liked her job.

Zack had decided not to tell Janet about the possible job offer. There was no need to upset her in case it
didn't come through. But as the opportunity became a
reality, he knew he had to tell her. He wrote for newspapers from the area where he might work. The housing
market looked good. He found want ads for jobs like
Janet now had. He knew church was important to her, so
he checked out churches in the community.

As Zack retraced both his steps and his thoughts, he
couldn't see why Janet was so angry. He had learned
something from their almost six years of marriage. He
had considered her needs too. He had it all there for her
to see that night—newspapers, church bulletins, pictures of houses. But she wouldn't look at any of it.

Once again he stood at the same corner. This time

he turned left and went home. He saw Janet still sitting at the table. The papers he had left had all been moved.

"I think I am sorry about something, but I haven't figured out what it is yet," Zack said. "So I came home to ask you."

She smiled. Home free!

"I'm sorry I blew my top, Zack," she said. "But I will let you know what you can be sorry about. You've spent four months thinking about making a major change in our lives—and you expected me to make the adjustment in four minutes. It's my marriage too. It's also my home, and it involves my job too. You had no right to plan all of this without talking to me. All this stuff that you gave me is important, but I should have been in on collecting it. I should have gotten to ask the questions instead of being here just to say yes or no."

Zack sat quietly for a moment. He had not learned as much in six years as he had thought. Or maybe he had, but he knew that he would always have more to learn.

"I'm sorry, dear," he said. "I thought I was doing the right thing and it made sense—even while I was circling the block out there. I just didn't want you to worry about something that might not have happened."

"But the worrying part belongs to both of us," she said. "I need time to adjust to new ideas. You took that away from me."

"Could we start over again—again?" he asked.

"Sure. What do you want to talk about?"

Prayer

> Lord God, we know we share a bed, a checkbook, and a table. Help us understand that we also share worries, joys, and hope. In Jesus' name. Amen.

Jacob was in love with Rachel, so he said, "I will work seven years for you, if you will let me marry Rachel."
Genesis 29:18

I'm Not in Love with You Anymore

"Hey, Bro, good to hear from you," Charlie said as he muted the TV.

"I'm glad I found you home," Ronnie replied.

"How's it going with you?"

"Not so bad, not so good."

"What's the part that's not so good?" Charlie asked. "Family okay?"

"Yeah, I finally got the kids to sleep," Ronnie answered. "Martha's out with the girls tonight."

"Good. Cindy has a meeting at church, so I'm kid-keeping too. We can talk."

"It's not so simple," Ronnie said. "After dinner tonight Martha told me she's not in love with me anymore."

"What?"

"Well, she said that she loves me, but she's not *in* love with me anymore."

"What does that mean?"

"I'm not sure," Ronnie answered. "I think it means she wants a divorce."

"But she said she loves you," Charlie reminded his brother.

"Sure," Ronnie said, "but she said it in a tone of voice that could have applied to her father—or the dog."

"Did you ask her what she meant?"

"We talked for a while. She said the excitement and romance has gone out of our marriage."

"Has it?" Charlie asked.

"We've been married seven years and have two kids," his brother answered. "I suppose the honeymoon is over."

"Sex life okay?"

"I thought so," Ronnie answered. "In fact, I thought it was great. I asked her. She said she had no complaints in that area. I guess I'd like to have gotten a little higher score than that, but I don't think the problem is in bed."

"Do you talk to each other—about real things?"

"Yes. In fact, last week I told her I thought she was hanging around with divorced and man-hating women too much. Tonight I told her they were the source of this 'I love you but I'm not *in* love with you' crap."

"What did she say?"

"She said I thought that because I hang around with divorced men and male chauvinists. By the way, she may have included you in that last category."

"We'll deal with that later," Charlie said. "What are you going to do?"

"I just needed to talk to someone tonight, Charlie," Ronnie said. "Tomorrow I am going to ask her to go with me to see the pastor or a marriage counselor."

"Good idea. And I'm glad you called me."

Prayer

Renew our love for each other each day
Like the morning dew. In Jesus' name. Amen.

Homework

Does your marriage need a 5,000-mile checkup? Who can help you evaluate your marriage? Do you know that most people who get divorces say they could have saved their marriage if they had asked for help sooner?

The love of money is a source of all kinds of evil. Some have been so eager to have it that they have wandered away from the faith and have broken their hearts with many sorrows. 1 Timothy 6:10

• •

The Dollar Market 1

A dollar is a dollar is a dollar. Or so it would seem. But there is an American dollar, a Canadian dollar, and an Australian dollar. Each has a different value. While the value of any one of those national dollars seems to stay the same (one hundred cents make one dollar), the value of each in relationship to the others changes daily.

So much for international finance. Let's look at family finances. The family also may have different values on a dollar. There is his dollar, her dollar, and our dollar. From day to day the value of each dollar may vary in relationship to the others.

He and she each need to know how each establishes the value of his or her own dollar. For example, how much is "a lot of money" to him? to her? What is the price for something that "doesn't cost very much"? Each person in a marriage needs to know what he or she means about the value of money. Each one also needs to know the other's value of a dollar.

The value of his dollar and her dollar can be seen in the way each expresses priorities. One will place a higher value on the dollar that is saved or invested. Another will place a higher value on a dollar that is spent on education, recreation, vacation, or hobbies. One would place a higher value on a dollar spent on a car, the other a higher value on the dollar spent on a home. One may place a high value on money given to church; the other may want to spend money on gifts for family and friends.

When his dollar and her dollar are used together they become our dollar. For the sake of the budget, both husband and wife must know the values of the dollars they use together. But in marriage this is more than a budget issue; it is a way of understanding values. Disagreements about money are really not about dollars and cents, but about priorities. His values tell him to spend money on what he thinks is important. Her values tell her to spend money on what she thinks is important. Discussions cannot be limited to financial issues such as these: Who made it? Who decides how it is spent? Instead, a couple must talk about ways to bring his values and her values in focus to be our values.

The process of making his dollar and her dollar into our dollar can be a great blessing in a marriage. It requires communication. First, each one must establish and understand his or her own values. Then each must communicate those values to the other. The management of money, therefore, becomes a secondary issue. The real issue is understanding: first understanding oneself, then understanding one's spouse.

Prayer

Heavenly Father, help us to see our money as a gift from You and to use it in partnership with You and one another, so we may enjoy life and be of value to our family and our community. In Jesus' name. Amen.

Each one should give, then, as he has decided, not with regret or out of a sense of duty; for God loves the one who gives gladly. And God is able to give you more than you need, so that you will always have all you need for yourselves and more than enough for every good cause.
2 Corinthians 9:7–8

The Dollar Market 2

Some husbands and wives operate with his dollar and her dollar and do not establish a mutual financial system for our dollar. In rare cases (such as when each partner has adult children from a previous marriage), that may be the best system. However, in most marriages, the process of learning to operate with a single budget requires a bride and a groom to talk to each other and to establish ways of working together that will help them in other areas of their marriage also. It's one process that helps brides and grooms to become wives and husbands.

In a joint budget both spouses contribute to the fund, and both can spend from it. The value of our dollar is not determined by who puts the most dollars into the fund. Too often the partner who makes the most money feels that he/she has a greater say in how the money is to be spent. In the total economy of a marriage, time is as important as money. One partner may put more money into the checking account, but the other may put more time into operating the household. The value of our dollar is, therefore, established by both. And both must understand the value of the money they have together.

Here's one simple way to help develop that understanding: Pretend that each spouse receives an unexpected and unrestricted gift of a thousand dollars. Each one writes down on a piece of paper what he or she would do with the thousand bucks. Then each writes down what he or she thinks the other would do with the same money.

Another way: Each one lists the following subjects according to financial priorities. The first item on your list is what needs the most money, the last needs the least. One more thing: Each spouse may add three items to the list given here.

Housing	Entertainment	Sports
Vacation	Food	Transportation
Church	Hobbies	Medical care
Taxes	Savings	Alcohol
Pets	Clothing	Personal grooming
Gifts	Eating out	Furniture

Compare the two lists, and you will see the difference between the value of his dollar and her dollar. And you will know what areas need discussion to make them become a part of our dollar.

Prayer

Lord, You have made the two of us become one.
Now please help us to make our time,
Our energy, and our money
Become one also.
In Jesus' name. Amen.

But you, my friends, already know this. Be on your guard, then, so that you will not be led away by the errors of lawless people and fall from your safe position.
2 Peter 3:17

* *

10th-Anniversary Surprise

"Darling! You got the exact same table!" Kay said in delight as she and her husband were ushered to the same table in the same restaurant where he had proposed to her over 10 years ago.

"I thought it was the perfect place to celebrate our 10th anniversary," Eric replied. "I made the reservation six weeks ago to make sure we got this table."

"Look, they've already put a bottle of our wine on ice," Kay said.

"Maybe we could have afforded a little better after 10 years," Eric said. "But I thought I'd stick with tradition."

After the two had sat down and ordered the same meals as on the night they became engaged, they tried to recall what they had done on each of their wedding anniversaries. Their memories were interrupted by the low but persistent voices of the couple at the table next to them. They could not avoid overhearing what was being said.

Eric could see the other couple. They were about the same age as he and his wife. They were well dressed, and from appearances could also have been celebrating a special event. But the tones of their voices and the words that Kay and Eric heard told a different story. First the strangers talked about joint custody of two children, agreeing that neither would move from the city. Then they discussed financial things: the sale of a home, the division of retirement accounts.

"I'm sorry, sweetheart," Eric said. "I thought I had planned a perfect evening. Shall we move to another table?"

"No," she answered. "It was romantic of you to think of getting this table. I want to stay here."

"But the background noise is not creating the mood I had planned," Eric protested. "I think it is rude for people to discuss such things in public."

"Don't you know why they are doing this?" Kay asked.

"Because they are getting a divorce and can't stand to be in the same house with one another."

"But that's not all," Kay said. "I read an article in a magazine while I was waiting for the dentist today. It said that people who work out the details of a divorce in a lawyer's or counselor's office pay over one hundred dollars an hour. If they do it at home, they get into an argument. So the writer suggested that couples go to an expensive restaurant where they have to follow the rules of society. There they can talk about all the details without yelling—and all it costs is the price of a dinner."

"Did the article have any suggestions for the people at the nearby tables?" Eric asked.

"No, but I do," Kay answered. "Let's thank God that we came here to celebrate. After 10 years some couples take each other for granted. I think we are getting a good reminder not to do that."

Prayer

Thank You, God, for the blessings we remember and the ones we might forget. In Jesus' name. Amen.

*How wonderful it is, how pleasant, for God's people
to live together in harmony! Psalm 133:1*

Routines

When a man and a woman become a husband and a wife, they develop routines. Some of these routines become so routine that the husband and wife don't even notice them anymore. They are like two figure skaters in the Olympics.

Watch how you and your spouse do certain routine things: getting in the car, going to bed, fixing lunch, making love. You know where the other one is. Each of you knows what to expect of the other. You are two acting as one.

First, recognize routines that include movement. Notice how one checks the locks on the doors, and the other turns off the lights. One gets the newspaper; the other makes coffee. One showers while the other brushes teeth.

Then look for the routines in the ways you think and feel. After a few years of marriage, your humor develops a routine, and the two of you laugh at something that others wouldn't understand. You develop a routine on things to worry about and what you pray about. You learn each other's emotional cycles. You either join each other in being elated or depressed, or you provide a balance so the other can be off balance for a while.

Often married couples do not recognize the many positive routines they have. The routines seem to come naturally, so they are taken for granted. Take time to identify the good routines that you have established in your marriage.

Not all husband-wife routines are positive. If couples with good routines are like figure skaters in the Olympics, those who have developed bad ones are like two people riding bumper cars at the county fair.

Watch for the things you do that make you bump into each other. Can the two of you work in the kitchen together? do income taxes together? shop together? Are there times when you and your spouse work together that you want to say, "If you would just get out of the way, I'd get this job done"?

Sometimes you may bump into each other literally—in the kitchen or in the bathroom. But that can be fun. Most of the bad routines develop when you bump into each other in ways you feel and ways you think.

Watch for routines in your marriage when you and your spouse are like bumper cars crashing into each other. Do you recycle the same misunderstandings, disagreements, arguments? Do certain events always cause conflicts in your marriage? For example, when the bank statements, credit card bills, and phone bills arrive? when you ride in the car in heavy traffic together? when you are late for a social or business appointment? when the car or household appliances break down?

Can you change the bad routines? Can one of you make the change, or will you need to work together? Recognizing and changing bad routines can become a good routine.

Prayer

Dear Jesus, help us see the good things in our marriage,
and help us change the things that hurt. Amen.

Cook me some of that tasty food that I like,
and bring it to me. Genesis 27:4

* *

Milk Gravy

Harry was eager to get home. He and Amy had lived in their own apartment for three weeks. For three weeks he had had a key, a daily newspaper, his toothbrush in place. But all of that was just the setting for the great drama of his life. He had a wife. Someone to kiss good-bye in the morning. Someone to greet him when he came home. Someone to hold close all night long.

And for three weeks he had been hungry.

Harry had not anticipated this problem. Amy had seemed to like to cook. She was happy when she got kitchen things as wedding gifts. She was especially proud of her cookbook collection. She liked using all of their new dishes and set the table in a beautiful way. She always got home an hour before he did, so dinner was ready when he came home.

She served salads. Each day a different kind of salad, tasty, obviously healthful, but short on substance. Once Harry almost slipped and said, "The salad was delicious, honey. I'll go get the rest of the meal."

But his wisdom won out over his humor. He realized his wife had prepared her own meals for three years. Now he knew why she had such a terrific figure. But in his family a meal included meat and potatoes.

Today Harry had a solution. He skipped lunch and got off work an hour early. Amy had told him she had a meeting after school, so she would be late. He had told her not to worry about dinner, and he knew she thought he would take her out. But he had a better plan.

He stopped at a supermarket. He wasn't sure what was available at home, so he bought what he needed: pork chops, potatoes, green beans, milk, and flour. No salad stuff.

Next he rushed home. He coated five pork chops with flour and put the potatoes in a pot to boil. He used another pot for the beans and set the table. He burned his fingers while trying to peel the cooked potatoes, but that was easier than doing it when they were raw. He watched the clock to time things just right. The potatoes were mashed and in the oven with the platter of pork chops.

Harry heard Amy's car. He stirred a large cup of flour in the pan with meat drippings. As he heard his wife coming up the steps, he poured the milk into the skillet. This was the meal he had seen his mother prepare many times.

He turned to greet his wife and enjoy the happy surprise on her face. He saw her look scared as she rushed past his open arms to the stove where she turned off the burner. He turned to see milk gravy running over the top of the skillet, into the burner, and down the side of the stove. That had never happened to his mother.

Amy was roaring with laughter. She picked up the sack of flour and said, "Good try, dear, but you bought self-rising flour."

Prayer

Bless the food we eat and the love that comes with it.
In Jesus' name. Amen.

Homework

Do you and your spouse enjoy the same foods? What can each of you do to make mealtime a happy time?

*People who listen when they are corrected will live, but
those who will not admit that they are wrong
are in danger. Proverbs 10:17*

● ●

Communication Check 5
Go for the Gold

Welcome to the graduate course in marriage communication! As in all education, the more you learn about communication in marriage, the more you realize how much you have yet to learn. This graduate-level course is called "Go for the Gold"—that is the gold of the golden anniversary, 50 years of marriage.

One of the big blocks to communication is this statement: But you do the same thing!

In conversations it works this way. One spouse becomes concerned about something the other has done or said. It may be something minor: mistakes in grammar or manners, the way one dresses, telling jokes that border on bad taste. Or it may be a more serious subject: misuse of alcohol, uncontrolled temper, matters of honesty, a need for counseling.

Whatever the subject, one spouse waits for the right time and situation to say to the other, "I think you are making a mistake about . . ."

And the other replies, "But you do the same thing!"

The conversation started with an effort by one to help the other. However, the but-you-do-the-same-thing defense changed the subject. The conversation now has two accusers and two defenders. The couple is now in a debate about who is the more guilty—and the conclusion will help no one. Or they are in a do-it-yourself courtroom scene with both on trial. And both will be found guilty.

The solution is simple, but takes discipline. *Agree to discuss only one spouse's faults at a time!* Be glad that you have someone who loves you and is close enough to you to notice if you are getting more than a half a bubble off on any situation. People often get sick (physically and emotionally) gradually. Those who become dangerously obese gained their weight one pound at a time. People develop eccentric or dangerous behavior patterns gradually. No one goes off the deep end suddenly—the individual works at it over a long period of time.

But the spouse will be the first to notice. If you are concerned about some pattern in your marriage partner's behavior, talk about it. But do not accuse. Instead, ask the spouse to examine himself/herself.

If your spouse asks you to look at yourself, don't defend yourself and don't attack your spouse. Someone who cares about you has shown concern for you.

The discussion will help you only if you listen to your spouse's concern. You may need to explain. You may need to ask questions. But you do not need to defend yourself. And you do not make yourself right by proving your spouse wrong. If your spouse does have a similar, or a different, problem, that's another subject—for another day.

Prayer
Lord, help us speak to one another on Station LOVE.
In Jesus' name. Amen.

Homework
Do you refuse to listen to your spouse speak about certain subjects? Do you think your spouse refuses to listen to you on any subject?

[The woman:] How handsome you are, my dearest; how you delight me! Song of Songs 1:16

[The man:] What a magnificent girl you are! How beautiful are your feet in sandals. The curve of your thighs is like the work of an artist. Song of Songs 7:1

● ●

Everyone Has a Beauty Spot

"Will you do something for me?" the man asked.

"What?" the woman answered.

"When I tell you how beautiful you are," he said, "I wish you would just say, 'Thank you,' instead of, 'No, I'm not.' "

"When I tell you that you are sexy," the woman answered, "you always try to deny it."

"Maybe that's because I want you to say it again and again," he answered.

"So maybe I want you to tell me that I am beautiful over and over again."

"On the other hand," the man said, "the facts are that I am short, overweight, and bald. None of those things are listed under sexy in the dictionary."

"If you want to get technical about it," the woman answered, "I've known that I am a Plain Jane ever since my ninth-grade science teacher thought I was a boy."

"But you are beautiful to me," he protested. "And sexy."

"And you are handsome in my sight," she said. "And sexy."

"You know," the man said, "when we make love I feel that way."

"So do I," the woman said.

"Why?"

"Because we love each other."

"But what about the cameras and mirrors?" he asked. "And the science teacher?"

"Love outranks them!" she said.

"Then we're not kidding ourselves?"

"Of course not," the woman said. "Everyone has a beauty spot. I see yours with no problem. But it amazes me that you see beauty in me."

"But your beauty is so obvious to me," the man said. "Everyone should be able to see it."

"I guess we're blessed," the woman said. "Some people have their beauty on the skin and in their shape. They look like they are sexy because they have over-standard equipment. Others may be so attracted to them that they don't look for the deeper beauty spots."

"I'm blessed to have you," the man said.

"And I'm blessed to have you," the woman answered.

"To hell with cameras and mirrors."

"And science teachers' opinions."

Prayer

> God, Creator of all that is,
> Thank You for giving beauty to me
> Through my spouse.
> Thank You for giving my spouse eyes
> That see beauty in me.
> In Jesus' name. Amen.

*If one part of the body suffers, all the other parts suffer
with it; if one part is praised, all the other parts share
its happiness. 1 Corinthians 12:26*

* *

A 5,000-Mile Checkup

"I missed lunch today because I had to wait a half-hour at the garage," Gary said as he reached for his third helping at dinner.

"Wasn't there a fast-food place in the neighborhood?" Fran asked.

"I wasn't in the mood for fast food," Gary answered. "Besides, I found something that interested me. There was a big sign that said, 'DOES YOUR CAR NEED A 5,000-MILE CHECKUP?' Next week is our wedding anniversary. I wonder if we need a 5,000-mile checkup?"

"If we do," Fran answered, "I certainly don't want to get it at Jimmy's Garage."

"No, this is a do-it-yourself project," Gary said. "Do you think our marriage is well tuned?"

"To be honest," she said, "I think you're a little pushy."

"Me, pushy?" he reacted. "I thought you were the pushy one."

"You were the one who kept stopping at jewelry store windows and asking what kind of engagement rings I liked—even before I agreed to marry you. That was pushy."

"I thought it was romantic," he said. "But I thought you were pushy when you told me all the places you wouldn't live and the kind of house you didn't want, before you agreed to marry me."

"I thought that was being assertive," she said. "But this is a 5,000-mile checkup—for what's happening now. You're still pushy when you always want to invite people over for dinner and always want to go visit other people."

"I think of that as being social," Gary answered. "I think you're pushy when you want to move the furniture all the time and buy things to cover every blank spot on the walls."

"That's interior decorating to me," Fran answered. "You seem to like the way our home looks. You always invite people over to see it."

"And you must want people to come; you always have something new to show to guests.

"I suppose a checkup has to be followed by a tune up," Gary suggested. "Would you be happier if I talked to you before I invited someone to our place or accepted an invitation for both of us?"

"Yes, I would," Fran said. "And would you be happier if I talked to you about what I bought for the house—and where it would be placed?"

"Yes," he said. "But just for the record, I'd rather you be pushy than mousy."

"Okay," she answered, "and I admit I'd rather you be pushy than dull."

"See, this checkup shows we're getting good mileage out of our marriage."

Prayer

*Lord Jesus, help each of us know what is happening
to the other one. Amen.*

Homework

What would you discuss in a 5,000-mile checkup of your marriage? Should you ask a pastor/counselor to help?

[Jesus said,] "Be concerned above everything else with the Kingdom of God and with what He requires of you, and He will provide you with all these other things."
Matthew 6:33

● ●

Toothpaste in the Drawer

It was February 14, and four men who rode in a car pool had stopped at a shopping center on the way home from work. The two men who sat in the back of the car each had a large heart-shaped box of candy. The driver, Jerry, had a small package from a jewelry store. Greg, the front-seat passenger, had a sack from a drugstore. In it were two tubes of toothpaste—tied together with a red ribbon and a small valentine.

"Hey, Greg, aren't you going overboard on being the romantic?" asked one of the men in the back seat. "I mean, you must have something special going if you can get away with giving your wife toothpaste on Valentine's Day."

"Candy's dandy, but toothpaste is cheaper," laughed the other rider in the back seat.

After the other two riders had been dropped off, Jerry said, "Maybe it's none of my business, Greg, but I've been around you and Dee, and I know you've got a good thing going in your marriage. The toothpaste does seem a little strange as a Valentine gift."

"I don't know what is in your package to Amy," answered Greg, "but I know Dee will enjoy the toothpaste more than a box of candy or a piece of jewelry."

"Sounds like there is a story I don't know," said Jerry. "And you don't have to tell me."

"I suppose I want to tell you because you know Dee," answered Greg, "but don't pass it on.

"Dee grew up poor, I mean in real, old-fashioned, industrial-strength poverty. Her mother had a lot of health problems, and her dad had only seasonal work. But they did the best they could.

"One of Dee's childhood memories is that they never had enough toothpaste. Every day she would try to squeeze one more dab out of the tube. And others in the family were doing the same thing to the same tube. Now, I know what it is like to squeeze the last bit out of a tube of toothpaste. But I did it because my mother forgot to buy more or because my brother and I had had a toothpaste war. Dee did it because there was no more toothpaste.

"We were married about five years before she told me that story. I felt so great that she trusted me enough to tell me. She knew I wouldn't laugh at her.

"Ever since then I sneak tubes of toothpaste into her drawer in the bathroom. You know that we're doing okay and live well. But her security comes from opening that drawer and seeing two, maybe three, big, unused tubes of toothpaste. She knows that I know what she really wants."

"You're a romantic old son-of-a-gun," said Jerry. "Dee's lucky to have you."

"No, I'm the one who is blessed," answered Greg. "She lets me love her. That helps me let her love me."

Prayer

Lord, help me know who I am
So I can explain me to my spouse.
And help my spouse be real to me.
In Jesus' name. Amen.